Alienated

A Quest to Understand Contact

by

Jeanne Marie Robinson

Introduction by Debbie Jordan Kauble

Greenleaf Publications
P.O. Box 8152
Murfreesboro, Tennessee 37133
USA

Manufactured in the United States of America

Library of Congress catalog card number
97-74545

ISBN
1-883729-05-X

To our children:
Make the world a kinder garden.
May you learn from our mistakes.
Love is the ultimate power of the universe.

*From a wild weird clime
That lieth, sublime
Out of Space—out of Time*

From "Dreamland" by Edgar Allen Poe

Contents

Preface   ix

Acknowledgments   xiii

Introduction   1

Chapter 1: Waking Up Is Hard To Do   3

Chapter 2: On the Edge of Sanity   9

Chapter 3: Discovery   17

Chapter 4: Through the Eyes of a Child   23

Chapter 5: Nightmare on Red Creek   29

Chapter 6: Rage   35

Chapter 7: Rainbow   39

Chapter 8: Davy Jones's Locker   45

Chapter 9: Communication Breakthrough   51

Chapter 10: The Crystal City   59

Chapter 11: The Baton Rouge Incident   65

Chapter 12: Psychoanalyzed   71

Chapter 13: Debbie and I   77

Chapter 14: Feeding Time   85

Chapter 15: Butterfly Dance   91

Chapter 16: New Friends   101

Chapter 17: Communication Breakdown   109

Chapter 18: The Dark Side   123

Chapter 19: Rebirth   133

Chapter 20: On the Edge of the Future   137

Chapter 21: Future Visions, Future Fears   143

Chapter 22: Winds of Change   149

Epilogue   157

Appendix A: Telepathic Communications   161

Appendix B: Transcript: Feeding the Babies   181

Appendix C: Inspiration   197

Index   209

Preface

Something is happening to me that I cannot explain.

It all began with a triggered awakening to what seemed to be one or more alien abductions. Hidden in my subconscious was a vast array of memories. Memories of experiences with large-eyed, small, humanoid beings conducting examinations aboard strange, flying craft. These memories are as real to me as any I have ever known. Recalling these incidents under hypnosis was an emotionally draining blend of trauma and wonder.

Over the last five years, I have tried without success to file these experiences in some comfortable category. I have broadened my understanding of what possibilities may exist. It is not just a repetitive UFO experience. There are elements of interdimensionality with religious/ spiritual overtones. The human psyche must also be taken into consideration. There may be an aspect of consciousness of which even psychologists are unaware.

I am only one of many. What is happening to me is happening to thousands of others. Many tell stories hauntingly similar to mine. We struggle daily to live normal lives while keeping our phenomenal secrets to ourselves. Fear of ridicule keeps us silent. Those who speak out are subjected to character assassination, the ridiculing laughter of the misinformed, and sometimes loss of employment. We are ordinary people who are having extraordinary experiences on a continuing basis.

I refuse to remain silent.

I don't know what it is that has intruded so easily into my life and turned it upside-down. I want answers. My experiences are both good and bad, both intriguing and terrifying. They could mean either the salvation or destruction of mankind or some other form of dualism yet unclear to me. I will no longer sit and suffer the weight of it alone. I will relate what I know of my own experiences to you, the reader. This is all I can do. Final evaluations are up to you.

In 1989 I began to undergo hypnotic regressions to recover my memories. Since then I have received much information and many thoughts through what seems to be a telepathic connection with something (or someone) other than myself. Without warning, my mind is flooded with information and commentary on a wide range of topics. I have written down many of these thoughts and saved them. Some are difficult, if not impossible, to understand. I hesitate to throw them away, though, because they might be of some use to someone.

The content of these communications has often implied that they are of an extraterrestrial origin. I do not have the vaguest idea where they come from. I also warn anyone reading this not to consider this information to be the "ultimate truth." I treat it as a quirky little byproduct of the abduction experience. I am sure it contains both lies and truths. I try not to take it too seriously, but I am intrigued by the strangeness of it all.

It will be obvious that I have alternately positive and negative feelings about what has happened to me. I have a love-hate relationship with these beings (whoever they are). If I understood their motives, I would be less indecisive in my feelings. That is the problem; no one knows—or is willing to share—the answer. I have settled on the opinion that both good and bad entities are involved. My dilemma becomes more difficult when I attempt to differentiate between the two.

These experiences have stretched the limits of my reality. In 1987, I was not very spiritual. Now something has changed within me. I am evolving. It is a slow and sometimes painful process, but I feel I am becoming a better person. There seems to be a reciprocal relationship between this heightened spiritual awareness and the extraterrestrial experiences. I am trying to understand both concepts.

I am presenting all the incidents as they have appeared to me, as truthfully as I am able. I do not claim to understand this experience, and I do not expect anyone else to understand it. It may be safer for you, the reader, to view this book as fiction. Be my guest. Contained within these pages is a special truth just for you. You will know when you have found it because you will feel it in your heart.

My life has been, and continues to be, a question. This book is my personal search for answers. Perhaps, in the process of writing it, I will reach some conclusions I can live with. In that respect, this endeavor is a form of therapy. It is a challenge and a quest for understanding. I hope I may share some of that understanding with each of you.

Acknowledgments

This book would never have been written without the faith and support I have received from countless individuals who have influenced my life in many ways. I will never be able to list them all. Even the smallest of synchronicities sometimes played a large part in the creation of this work.

First and foremost, I thank my family for the love and support they have given me throughout my turbulent life. Even though we have different viewpoints and beliefs, my family has always provided a loving environment. Words fail to express the gratitude I feel. Thank you for the love, laughter, and the strong foundation of faith that has helped me survive all the uncertainties.

I want to thank my editors and publishers at Greenleaf Publications for giving me the opportunity to express myself and share my experiences with others. Leah Haley and Marc Davenport have been instrumental in bringing this information to the public. So much of the UFO information in this country is placed in the governmental "need-to-know" category. I feel it is time for public honesty, and I believe everyone has the right and the need to know that other intelligent life forms and influences are affecting this planet.

Thanks to Debbie Jordan Kauble for her insight, friendship, and understanding, and for sharing her home with my daughter and me. The time we spent at the farm will always be a special memory, and has helped me find the strength I needed to get back on my feet after the "fear year."

Many thanks to Budd Hopkins for his work in abduction research, and for sending me information that enabled me to contact my hypnotherapist. That is one synchronistic event that changed my life. Many people are having similar experiences who have no avenue of closure and no professional or emotional assistance to help lessen the stress and fear that comes from the unknown. The need for strong, honest, ethical support should be addressed by the psychological community.

I would like to thank the Springfield, Missouri, research and abductee support group for their help and friendship. We search for understanding of a greater reality, and are able to find comfort in the bond we share. To be able to talk openly about our experiences is a great blessing.

Thanks to Nadine Bartlett for giving me emotional support when I nervously told her of my "symptoms" of contact. She was the first person I spoke to about my experiences, and she has been a great friend to me throughout the last ten years.

I want to thank Linda Moulton Howe for giving me an avenue of expression when I needed to speak out and share the information I had been given. Linda also listened and offered support during the phase when I was plagued by fears and uncertainties.

I want to thank Duane and Susan Bedell for their friendship and for inviting me and others into their home. I appreciate the help they have given me in preparation for this book.

Thanks to Jean Brogan for friendship and laughter, and for having faith in me when I had no faith in myself.

Thanks to Vince Serencko for our adventures in UFO research and for help on computer problems. His knowledge of the history of ufology has helped me understand my part of the "bigger picture."

I want to thank the Moody Blues for the uplifting music that warms my soul and helps me believe love can make the future a brighter place for us all.

For the gang at Bones, who were the first to hear me sing, thanks for the encouragement and for keeping me laughing. You are a fine example of how diversity can be harmonious.

I want to express unending gratitude to all the people who have touched my life and made it richer. It is impossible to personally thank you all individually, but it is important to me that you know how much you have helped me to grow stronger (and, I hope, wiser).

I have met many friends who prefer to remain anonymous. To all the experiencers who are having incredible incidents in their lives and prefer to avoid the public meat grinder, I understand the fear of ridicule. I hope that someday we can all be treated respectfully and honestly. It is this dream that has given me the strength to speak out. This book is written for you with love.

Introduction

Have you ever met someone and, instantly, you knew there was something very special about that person? That's how it was for me the first time I met Jeanne Robinson.

I cannot remember who actually sent the first letter. I suspect our letters crossed in the mail. Both of us were very excited about getting to meet the other. We exchanged several letters before we had an opportunity to meet face to face.

We were brought together by a couple of researchers with whom we had both been working. They apparently noticed many similarities in our cases, and perhaps thought it might be a "hoot" to see what would happen if they put the two of us together (in the name of research, of course). I will always be grateful to them for helping me find one of the best friends I have ever had! Little did Jeane and I know, at the first meeting, just how intertwined our lives would become.

It became immediately apparent that Jeanne and I were destined to meet. The first time I looked into her eyes, I could see "the light" (what some of us "abductees" refer to as that part of someone we recognize—the part that tells us we have all shared the same incredible experiences). It was soon obvious to the researchers that they had stumbled onto something as they watched Jeanne and me interact. As if we were identical twins, we finished each others' sentences and seemed to be able to communicate with each other on a much higher level than speech permits. For Jeanne and me, it was exhilarating and awesome! It was something we always knew existed—something we had waited a long time to find.

Eventually Jeanne and her daughter came to live with my family and me. Living with someone gives one insight into the mind of that person in ways that nothing else can. While living with Jeanne, I came to learn that she is one of the most intelligent people I have ever known. This is a woman of extraordinary talent and strength, even if she sometimes fails to believe that about herself. (Her genuine humility and modest demeanor are refreshing, and only strengthen her credibility.)

What Jeanne has written in this book is as real as it gets. She has a way of expressing herself that allows the reader to truly feel what she has felt. You aren't reading her book, you are re-living her life through her work. I guarantee it will open your eyes—and perhaps your heart —in ways you never thought possible. Perhaps you will come to respect her and care for her as I have. And I hope you will find answers to a few of your own questions.

————Debbie Jordan Kauble
May 23, 1997

Chapter 1
Waking Up Is Hard To Do

I might never have known what memories were hidden in my subconscious, had I not picked up an *Omni* magazine in December 1987. Something drew me to the cover illustration and the mention of "missing time." I had never read *Omni* before, but I bought that particular one. It was my first experience with the "Triggering Effect." The article I read triggered something in my mind to begin remembering my own experiences.

The article discussed Budd Hopkins' book, *Intruders*. It addressed the connection between episodes of missing time and UFO abductions. Along with the article was a questionnaire for anyone who had seen a UFO or experienced missing time. Missing time was a term Mr. Hopkins used for any episode in a person's life during which time has passed but the person has no conscious recollection of events. An example might be a drive in the country that would normally take one hour but takes three hours instead, and, following the incident, the driver has no conscious memory of the extra two hours.

I had a conscious memory of seeing in the sky an unusual object that I could not identify as a conventional aircraft. Because of this incident, I decided to complete the questionnaire. As I did so, more and more of the questions seemed to apply to me.

One concerned unusual scars or markings on the body. My mind immediately flew to a deep pit in my left arm that had always been explained as a vaccination scar. Suddenly that explanation seemed ridiculous. The scar was not in an area normally used for vaccinations, and it was much too deep.

Other questions asked about irrational fears of specific places, visits by the "Boogey Man," and unusual phobias. All of these applied to me. I was inexplicably nervous about a particular stretch of road near my home, and I was fearful of looking out windows at night.

By the time I finished the questionnaire, my mind churned with flashes of memory. Once, when I was a child, I saw a small being at the foot of my bed. Another time, I was lost in the woods and was chased by a large pig that helped me find my way home....

I wrote a long letter to Budd Hopkins, attached it to the completed questionnaire, and mailed them both.

In the months that followed, I could not force myself to forget what I had begun to remember. I bought *Communion* by Whitley Strieber and Hopkins' book *Intruders*. *Communion* was interesting and a bit frightening. I felt very uneasy when I read Strieber's description of a long-limbed, praying-mantis-like being.

Intruders affected me differently. I felt immediately drawn to "Kathie Davis," the subject of Hopkins' book. She seemed very real to me, and I could relate to all her feelings expressed in the book. I sat in my bedroom, reading and wishing I could talk to her. I was sure I would never have an opportunity to do so. I lived in a rural area of the Ozark Mountains, and was unlikely to do any traveling. Even the likelihood of Hopkins answering my letter seemed remote.

I was born in Branson, Missouri, long before it was the "Country Music Mecca" of the 1990s. I seemed to have had a fairly normal early childhood. Adolescence hit me hard, however, and I grew to be a very troubled and rebellious teenager. I was extremely promiscuous and contemptuous of authority. I began to stay out all night and eventually made several attempts at running away from home. I have been a runaway ever since. I felt I had to leave the town where I grew up; it was unbearable for me. I did not realize, then, that you carry your troubles with you when you go.

I was still troubled by my memories, and when I finished reading *Intruders* and noticed the author's address in the back, I sat down and penned another long letter to Mr. Hopkins. I sealed the envelope, dropped it in the slot at the post office, and was immediately seized by an overwhelming feeling of remorse.

"You idiot!" I thought to myself. "Do you realize what you are doing? Sending a letter to a stranger, telling him you think you have been abducted by aliens? You have lost your mind!" This last idea began to seem like a distinct possibility.

Despite my misgiving, I wrote yet another letter to Mr. Hopkins not long after that. In it I listed a few additional memories that had surfaced. Once again I regretted having mailed the letter as soon as it dropped into the box. By then, however, I realized there was nothing more to say—at least until I got a response to my earlier correspondence.

Time passed and I received nothing.

Finally, almost a full year later, I received a form letter thanking me for completing the questionnaire. It included an address where I might write to get the results of the questionnaire. There was also a list of UFO-related books. I was upset. I did not need to read any more books! I needed some answers and some help. It seemed obvious to me that Mr. Hopkins had written me off as some kind of weirdo, and the form letter was a polite way of saying so.

I tried to forget my feelings and anxiety. Maybe I was a little crazy after all. I had had some rough moments in my life that were definitely unconventional and far from what I perceived as normal. The hardest part was not knowing. My mind would occasionally drift back to the disturbing memories, and I would unconsciously touch the pit in my arm, as if to rub it away.

One day in April 1989, I went to pick up my mail, and in my mailbox was a form letter from Budd Hopkins! He had not forgotten me at all. I learned later that he had been swamped by correspondence from a great many people as troubled as I was. It took him two years to work through the pile and get an answer to me. In the letter was general information on the use of hypnotic regression to recover memories and an explanation of what to expect from hypnosis. There was a warning that what I might discover in the process could change my life forever. That, I came to learn, was an understatement!

At the bottom of the letter was a personal note from Budd apologizing for the delay in replying and giving me the address of a hypnotherapist in my area. This last bit of information surprised me; I didn't think anyone in my part of the world would be interested in this UFO stuff—particularly not someone qualified to perform the hypnotic regressions I needed.

The letter created a brand new quandary. I had long ago written myself off as a bit crazed, and now I was faced with the opportunity to find out for sure. Now I was not sure I really wanted to know the answer. The therapist mentioned in the letter—I'll call him "Bill Johnson," lived in a city only 40 miles away. I could easily travel that far.

At work I began to drop hints about the subject of UFOs to my friend Nadine. I needed to talk to someone, and I wasn't ready yet to tell my family that I thought I was being abducted by aliens. Nadine seemed genuinely interested in the subject and recounted a sighting she had once had. I felt at last that I could confide my secret. That night we went for a drive to a nearby town. I began to tell her of all my suspicions and odd memories. As we drove, I told her about my letters and the reply. We discussed everything at great length and she suggested I give hypnotic regression a try, just to see what might happen.

I went home and wrote a letter to Mr. Johnson. Being the chicken that I am, I was not yet ready to make a phone call. Once again I felt like a complete idiot for contacting someone about a subject so bizarre. I was not happy with the first letter, and I tossed it into the trash. Then, I wrote:

Dear Mr. Johnson,

Hi. I received your address in a letter from Budd Hopkins. It was in response to letters I had written him on possible UFO experiences.

I wrote you one letter and tore it up. I would like to find out what happened or didn't happen to me, but it's a scary decision. For one thing, it might be a waste of time for both of us. Or I could be an abductee—or I could be looney-tunes. It's not the easiest thing to face.

I wish you would send me any information on what you do as an investigator and what I should expect if I explore this further. Do you keep things confidential? That's extremely important to me. I think I would like to meet with you and discuss it if possible. I am off nights and weekends (usually) and I only live about 40 miles away, so it wouldn't be a problem for me to get there.

Thanks for your help.

Sincerely,
Jeanne Robinson

Despite my misgivings, I mailed the letter.

One or two evenings later, the telephone rang. I found myself speaking to Bill Johnson. I had not given him my phone number, so I was surprised. Evidently, he had called Information for my number. I stuttered an embarrassed hello and listened as Bill introduced himself and gave me some background information. He asked me to tell him of a few of the things that were bothering me.

Over the next ten minutes the fears, memories, and anxieties poured out of me. I must have sounded like a raving lunatic. Bill seemed very nice and did his best to put me at ease. He told me he would send me a questionnaire to fill out. This would give him an idea of my feelings and would cover a bit of my personal background.

"Oh, joy" I thought sarcastically, "another questionnaire!"

Nevertheless, when the paper arrived, I filled it out. It was a list of a few psychological questions and some questions concerning books or movies I might have seen about UFOs and other strange phenomena. Eventually Bill and I agreed upon a time and place to perform the hypnotic regression.

This first meeting began a relationship that changed my life forever. Although the changes have been both positive and negative, I have never regretted that first step toward discovering who I really am. Spiritual as well as physical growth is essential for all of us. While there are limits to the physical, the potential for spiritual growth, whether fully realized or not, is enormous. As with all such things, no two people are exactly alike; different people progress at different rates. While I had grown physically, my spiritual growth had been diverted and plagued by confusion. Now it was my time to begin the journey.

Chapter 2
On the Edge of Sanity

I arrived early for my first hypnosis session. Feeling very nervous, I drove by the office Bill Johnson used for these occasions and pulled into a parking lot a block away. I sat and chain-smoked as I waited for the time of our appointment. When I could no longer put off the inevitable, I drove back to the small, brick building, pulled into the office parking lot, and waited.

Bill's appearance was different than I expected. I thought he would be older, although I'm not sure why. This young man in a T-shirt and tennis shoes seemed rather easygoing and non-threatening. I began to relax. We introduced ourselves, went inside his office, and began to discuss what I might want to explore under hypnosis.

There were several directions we could take. For example, there was the night I saw a "broken man" at the foot of my bed. (That was my way of describing a skull or skeleton when I was a very young child. I remembered waking up to see this thing in my bedroom.) I also mentioned a time when I got lost in the woods and was chased by a pig. I told Bill it was unusual for me to get lost because I knew the woods very well. The incident seemed weird, but I was not sure if anything about it fit into the UFO category. I had a vague memory of jumping a barbed-wire fence (to get away from the pig) and cutting my calf, just below the knee, on the barbed wire. We discussed these and numerous other occurrences as possible subjects for investigation.

After a bit more discussion about the hypnotic state itself, we began the session. Bill assured me that I would still have control of myself while in a trance. I was not sure I could be hypnotized, so it took a while for me to relax.

Gradually I began to see the wooded area I had walked through on the day I had gotten lost. As it became clearer, I described the direction I had taken that day. The scene seemed very clear to me now. I remembered an uprooted cedar that I had once fallen from and sprained an ankle. In my mind's eye, I walked on, describing the scene. Then, it suddenly seemed as if a screen were pulled over my eyes. I could not see anything beyond that point.

Bill decided to try another approach. He suggested I move forward to the time when I emerged from the woods and was chased by the pig. I began to describe the pig, the shape of which was rather unclear to me. I said it had large eyes and was taller than a pig should be. I began to feel very uneasy.

Bill asked me to see how I got to that point in the woods. In my mind, I turned to look back the way I had come—and once again the screen came up over my eyes. I could not see any further. I was filled with anxiety and frustration because we were getting nowhere. I knew there was more to the incident than what I had related, but, for some reason, I could not recall it.

Bill realized I was not going to remember anything. If there was anything there, it would remain hidden in my mind for at least one more night. He brought me out of the trance.

I was very frustrated that I could not remember. I just knew there was something there. I felt embarrassed that I had wasted Bill's time, but he assured me that it was okay and that the memories might surface later. He said there might be something there and there might not; we would just have to wait and see.

The next week was a crazy one for me. At odd moments, I experienced brief flashes of memory—jumbled images. I felt tremendous anxiety. My fear of looking out dark windows was incredibly strong, and I was very jumpy. I did not sleep much at night. Nadine kept a close watch on me at work during the daytime. I had a tendency to drift off into "Memoryland." This was not a good thing for someone responsible for operating machinery. I could not understand why I had easily remembered trivial details, and yet forgotten what had frightened me.

One night shortly after the session, I was just dropping off to sleep when suddenly I saw a sharp mental image of what seemed to be a large-eyed creature. I was wide awake instantly. The entity had sharp teeth—or something that looked like teeth! Although the image faded within seconds, it was very frightening.

I wrote to Bill:

May 27, 1989

Dear Bill,

I wanted to give you some details on the images I've been getting. I saw the face that I couldn't quite see the other night. I wasn't trying to remember anything. Whamo! I saw it as clear as a photograph! It wasn't like any of the pictures I had seen, but there were some similarities. The main difference was around the mouth...I think it was actually some kind of mask or something worn over the lower part of the face. What I thought at first was a small mouth with some nasty teeth, must've been a...vent or something.

The eyes were big and dark.... The image was only there for about two seconds. I didn't catch the surroundings, but it seemed to be inside somewhere that was dimly lighted. Like an old shed or something, that had bits of light trickling in (like through cracks or a partially covered window). I sensed a lot of junk or stuff around. Some cluttered up room. I didn't realize what I was seeing at first.

Just as I realized it was there, it turned its head toward me, and we made eye contact. Bill, that was the coldest damn stare you could ever imagine! You have heard of people "looking daggers"? This was "looking icicles." This thing scared me to death! The fear I felt when it looked at me was the same fear I had felt on those occasions I had looked out the window in the dark. This was what I didn't want to see looking back at me. The eyes looked like the same type of material that crawfish or shrimp eyes are made of. The coldness of the stare is what got to me. It was the same type of stare you might feel from a shark's eyes when it's about to have you for lunch.

Like I said, I got this all from about a two-second flash. Those two seconds gave me a shot of adrenaline that would kill a horse!

Wednesday night I stopped at a stoplight just as the light turned amber. The color combination of the orange-yellow and red lights gave me a flash of standing under something large with lights of a similar color. The height of the traffic light (several feet higher than my head) seemed to match the height of these other lights. I had the same feeling a day or so later when following a truck with lights of the same colors.

I know I mentally avoided some touchy areas [during hypnosis]. I saw everything clearly around the waterfall and creek, but as soon as I turned up the hill away from it, I felt my defenses start to set in. You kept urging me on, and I didn't want to go. I think something happened at that clearing. I also had a problem with censoring myself. I had flashes of things, and several times, instead of telling you, I told myself, "You didn't really see that." or "You're making that up." I kept it to myself. I think this comes from the fact that for two years I have wondered about this stuff and had a bad fear that I had a short circuit in my brain, causing me to make this all up for some crazy reason. I think this was a bit of self-defense, too. If I didn't say anything about it, we could bypass some touchy areas...

[During hypnosis] When you asked where I went next, I looked over at the end of the clearing (to where I thought I had gone) and had a glimpse of someone or something over there. That's when I told myself, "You didn't see that." That's when I put the wall up that made me block out where I went next. It wasn't that I *couldn't* remember; I *wouldn't* remember. You moved me on to when I saw the pig. I thought that was a semi-safe area because I had a pretty good memory of the pig. I remember looking behind me and it was like there was a wall up behind me, too. Like whatever was bad was behind me at that point. When you started asking me what the pig looked like, I couldn't really see it anymore. I had the old memory, but it kind of dissolved. That bothered me. You asked me to describe the face and did that counting backward from three. I wanted you to stop counting, but you didn't. So, when I had to see it, I didn't want to, so I blocked it. Or I filtered it or scrambled it so that I didn't have to see it. The eyes came through anyway. Didn't I say, then, that the eyes were cold or something similar?

When I told you about running and jumping over the fence, it really didn't seem clear. Like I didn't see me doing it. I didn't really see it happen. I looked at my arms and legs and I wanted to see the cut somewhere besides where I suspected it to be. Instead, I saw it where my scar was. I don't believe I saw my pants ripped where the cut was. Like it cut me without tearing my pants?

If I actually did meet up with the thing I saw, then it's going to be a hell of a job to get me to face it! I can see now why I was avoiding it...

I finished the letter and mailed it. The scar I was concerned about was a small, straight-line scar behind and slightly below my right knee. Recently I discovered that my sister Sharon has a similar scar in the same area of her right leg, behind the knee. It is in virtually the same spot as mine. Mine is horizontal and hers is vertical.

Several nights later, I awoke to use the bathroom. I looked at the clock; it was 3:10 AM. As I was returning to bed, my smoke alarm activated with a loud, piercing *peepeepeepeepeepeep* sound. It was longer and louder than the sound it makes when the battery charge is low. It did not continue as it would have had there been a fire. It scared the hell out of me. I looked down the hall where the alarm was located. Blue flashes of light were coming from my daughter's bedroom.

I knew I should check to see if there was a fire, and I was filled with a strong sense of panic. I tried to leave my bedroom but could not move through the door. It was as if I were physically restrained, but no one was there. I told myself, "You've got to check on Erin! There may be a fire!" Yet, I could not make myself go through that door.

At this point, a thought/voice in my head said, "*Lie down and go to sleep.*" Even though I was filled with fear and worry for my daughter, I walked over and lay down on the bed, the whole time berating myself for being a lousy mother. I should have checked out her room, but I couldn't. By this time, my adrenaline was flowing at a peak level.

I was lying on the bed. A tapping sound began. It sounded as if something were striking the outside wall of the trailer, near where I was lying inside. The sound continued at intervals. I looked and noticed a blue, flashing light shining in my window. It was similar to the flashing of police lights and identical to the flashes I had seen coming from Erin's room. Our local police vehicles' flashers are red, not blue.

The tapping continued until I thought I would go crazy. I thought, "Stop it please; please stop it!" I remember thinking they were after Erin this time. Who they might be did not occur to me. That is the last I remember. One minute I had peak adrenaline flow; the next minute I was waking up with the clock showing 4:10 AM! Everything was quiet and normal.

I remember thinking, "It's okay; they're gone now." Then I lay back down and went to sleep.

The next morning, Erin, who had just turned nine a week or two earlier, came into my room. I asked her if she had heard the smoke alarm during the night. She said she had, and told me of a dream she had had that night. She said, "There was a snake king and a mother looking for her two lost children."

I immediately called and left a message on Bill Johnson's answering machine.

Bill returned my call later that night, and I frantically told him everything that had happened the night before. He said not to worry; with all the stuff I had been thinking about, I had probably just scared myself.

I wasn't quite convinced of this, and I asked Bill if we could attempt hypnosis again. I felt sure something would come out this time. I told him that I felt the reason I did not allow myself to remember was because I had held everything in for so long. I was afraid to loose the fear because I might never gain control of it again.

We decided to try hypnosis again the following Wednesday. I knew something unusual was happening to me. The episode of the previous night was proof. It had not been my imagination, and now it involved my child. I was ready to face it, whatever it might be.

Chapter 3
Discovery

I arrived at Bill's office twenty minutes early.
My nerves were rampaging. I smoked one cigarette after another and
watched busboys empty trash behind the Mexican restaurant next door.
Once again I felt self-conscious about seeing a psychotherapist.

"I wonder if they know why I'm here?" I asked myself.

Bill arrived at the appointed time. We greeted each other as I
grabbed the foam pad I was using for a "psychiatrist's couch" during
hypnosis. I hurried inside, hoping no one noticed me. I felt conspicu-
ous, as if a neon sign were flashing "WEIRDO" above my head.

Bill began to ask me about the strange occurrences that had happened during the past week, and we discussed plans for the evening's
hypnosis session. Bill asked me what area I felt most compelled to explore. I mentioned several, including the UFO sighting I had experienced a few years earlier. I also felt strongly about trying again on my
walking-through-the-woods episode. I explained my fears of losing
control. Bill assured me he could include suggestions that would make

the memories less traumatic. I could view them as if through the eyes of a third person or a camera, in order to recall the events without distress.

I made myself comfortable on the mat, while Bill set up his tape recorder. Despite his assurances, I was still anxious about what might occur. I knew that the incidents I had begun to remember must be very scary for my mind to have fought so hard to not remember.

Bill began his induction procedure by suggesting I relax and free my mind of all the stresses of the day. He told me to concentrate on relaxing my entire body, beginning with my toes and working my way up. After I had achieved this relaxation, he told me to envision a very peaceful place—somewhere I felt safe and comfortable. I imagined a scene of a summer day in a nice meadow filled with flowers and butterflies, and with a few horses grazing nearby.

After allowing me to spend a few moments in this quiet place, Bill asked me to remember the front of the house in which I grew up. I described the simple stucco building as I remembered it, the front door with the coleus vine growing next to it. Bill asked me to take him on a tour of the place, and I proceeded to describe it, room by room.

He then asked if anything scary had ever happened there. I began to recall a night when, as a child, I awoke to find a skeleton or "broken man" at the foot of my bed.

I first saw its eyes. A small figure with large, black eyes was staring at me from the foot of my bed! I tried to cry for help, but I found I could not make a sound. I wanted to hide under the blanket to get away from the thing, but I was unable to move.

I next recalled lying naked on a cool, plastic-like table. I was no longer in my bedroom. I could not remember how I got to the table. Several of the pale, dark-eyed creatures were around me. I began to cry for my mother. I felt a pinch on my right arm and turned my head to see a metal hand holding me still. On my other side, one of the beings stood next to another robot-like hand that held a sharp instrument. I began to panic!

Bill calmed me down. He told me I could view the scene as if I were looking through a movie camera. He told me I was safe and that I had survived whatever it was that had happened.

Bill asked me to look at the creature and describe it. It was only a little taller than I was at that time—between four and five feet. Its deep-black, shiny eyes were the predominate feature of its face. I felt I was being drawn into them. It had no external nose—only two nostril slits close below the eyes. It had only a slit for a mouth, which never seemed to move.

"They look like ants!" I cried. "White ants!"

The skin on the creature seemed smooth and pasty white. The hands looked smooth and rubbery, with three fingers and a thumb and no nails. They looked similar to hands inside surgical gloves. There was no obvious bone structure, and no evidence of knuckles on the fingers, which appeared very flexible.

After I described this scene, Bill asked me what happened next. I began to cry and whimper. In my mind's eye, the mechanical hand came up and began cutting into my left arm with a metal instrument.

I began to squeal and cry harder, "Ow, it hurts! It burns! Mother! Mommy! Help me! Owww!"

The mechanical arm continued its work. The large-eyed creature stood by and observed the procedure. In my mind, I heard a voice "telling" me that I would be okay in a minute. I was four years old and experiencing trauma that was incredibly painful. Nevertheless, once I was "told" that I would be okay, I calmed down. The entire time this was happening, I never saw any blood. There was only a rhythmic cutting motion as tissue was removed and taken away.

As I related the event, I grabbed Bill's hand. It was as if I had to hold on to some link to the normal world while reliving this incident. This was something I had been denied when the original experience had occurred. One minute I was a normal child asleep in bed; the next minute I was in the middle of a living nightmare. I did not realize I was squeezing Bill's hand to a state of numbness until after the session.

Finally the painful procedure was finished, and I was allowed to sit up on the table. Another creature entered the room. He looked like the others but radiated a warm friendliness. Bill asked me to describe him. I told him it was "Grandpa."

"You mean it's your Grandpa?" Bill asked.

"No, he just feels like a grandpa."

He seemed old and comfortable, and I was no longer afraid. This being began to "speak" to me telepathically. His mouth did not move and I didn't actually hear a sound, but I clearly knew he was "speaking" to me in my mind. He told me not to be afraid, and that he would see me again from time to time.

I sat on the table with this small humanoid "grandpa" beside me. I noticed a hallway adjoining the room. Down the hallway came two small, bouncing lights.

"Ooh, puppies!" I giggled.

I don't know why I called them that. The lights seemed playful, like two puppies bounding after each other. They looked like Fourth-of-July sparklers without the stick. I began to notice the room around me. It was round, white, and spotlessly clean. It reminded me of a sterile doctor's office. The hallway connected to the room was long and curving. All along the outer wall were long, oval windows that stretched from a few feet above the floor almost to the ceiling.

"Grandpa" said, "Would you like to go home now?" I nodded to him that I was very much ready. The next thing I knew, I was back in my bed. I called to my parents in the next room, and they came in to check on me. I told them there had been a "broken man" in the room. They said I had a bad dream and I should go back to sleep.

As I calmed and relaxed into the sleep of a child, Bill decided to take me further. He asked me if I had seen this creature again. I told him I had seen it in the woods. I began to describe the area of woods I had walked through the day I got lost.

I walked up a hill that was rocky and covered with fallen leaves. I had never gone in that particular direction before that day. I was about twelve years old and very much a tomboy. I topped the hill and walked a little farther. Then, from behind a tree, stepped a little person (like the ones I had described above). I was very frightened as the first entity was joined by another. They "escorted" me farther into the woods. I saw yet another creature digging in the soil by a nearby tree. It seemed not to notice me. I was taken to a clearing at the top of the hill.

What I saw next took my breath away. It was the most beautiful object I had ever seen! It was a metallic vessel, hovering above the trees at the edge of the clearing. No sound came from it, and it appeared to be just sitting in the air. It was huge and triangular—like a silver manta ray. It seemed to be made of a shiny, silver-gray material like stainless steel. I was so filled with awe that I forgot my fear. The shape and beauty of it calmed me. It appeared to have black windows near the domed top. I could not take my eyes away from this beautiful machine that gleamed in the sunlight.

What was happening to me? I had never seen a craft like this before. It was magnificent! Who were these creatures? The only explanation I could think of was that all these things were from another world. What else could they be?

The little humanoids led me into the shadows beneath the ship and stepped back away from me. A beam of purplish-pink light engulfed me. I could see nothing around me but a swirl of colors similar to static on a television screen between channels. I felt a vacuum draw me upward; I was literally being "sucked" upward into the ship. I saw only a dark hole above me.

My next memory was of lying naked on a table once again. I was surrounded by the large-eyed entities. I felt my fear return. The table began to move and change. My feet came up and spread apart, leaving me terribly vulnerable to these odd creatures. I felt the metal clamp on my arm again. There was a strong cramping sensation in my belly. It felt as if someone were pressing something into my lower abdomen.

I cringed as the beings spread my legs apart. They pressed something into my vagina as I squirmed on the table. I felt totally violated. I was naive and didn't realize that anything could be put into me like that. I was terrified and alone. There was no one to save me from these strange visitors that had captured me. I felt horrified that their dark eyes were staring at my naked body. My stomach was cramping as the instrument was moved inside me. I lay there, sobbing, while these silent, alien "doctors" worked on me. The object was removed, and the creature moved to a work area on the other side of the room.

The next memory I had was of being returned to the woods. I was in my clothes and in an unfamiliar area. I felt dazed and disoriented. I walked down into a ravine and up another hill. I slowly regained my awareness as I looked around.

"I'm lost!" I thought, as I continued to walk.

I headed in what I hoped was the right direction. My stomach was still aching, and I began to feel hungry. Through the trees, I saw a shed that belonged to my neighbors. I climbed over a fence and looked behind me. A large pig stood looking at me for a moment, then ran into the trees. I felt a sore spot on my leg behind my knee. I must have cut it on the barbed wire, I thought.

I returned to my grandmother's house feeling strange. I was a bit irritated because I hadn't been missed. I remember thinking, "I was lost in the woods and nobody seems to care." But I often spent hours in the woods, and this absence would not have seemed unusual to my family. I was surprised that it was nearly noon. I had started my walk at about 9:30 in the morning.

Bill began to bring me out of hypnosis. He began to count backward from 20. I slowly opened my eyes and felt a little confused about where I was. Then it hit me. I just sat there for a minute.

"Wow!"

I looked at Bill and felt a big lump in my throat. The realization of what I had remembered was more than I could comprehend at that moment. I was unable to verbalize what I was feeling.

Bill asked me to try and draw the creatures I had seen. I penciled a rough sketch, but was too tired to go into much detail. I felt drained.

We spoke for a while about all the events I had recalled. It was so amazing to me. I had seen everything so crystal clear in my mind. It surprised me that all the memories had been so vivid. I knew I would be able to draw some of what I had seen. The images were very distinct.

"What do I do now?" I asked.

"Go home and get some rest." Bill told me. "Draw anything you can remember."

I took my mat and walked out to my car. I looked up at the stars. Which one did you guys come from? I wondered. And when are you coming back?

Chapter 4
Through the Eyes of a Child

The next morning I went to work, as usual. During my first break, I found myself drifting off into the memories. I went over the details again and again. My friend Nadine gave me a swift kick under the table. It was her subtle way of letting me know I was spacing out a little too much. I'd managed to tell her some of what had transpired.

I was running my machine, and the monotony of the job was conducive to subconsciously drifting off into my thoughts. Many memories were trying to surface. I wondered if I had opened a Pandora's box of suppressed experiences. I felt more excited than anxious. There was much to learn.

That day we ate lunch outside because it was warm and sunny. I felt a joy and a newness to life—a feeling that had been forgotten in my adulthood. I still felt the freshness of being four years old as I watched a butterfly fly by my face and land on the picnic table where I was sitting. I felt as if I were seeing everything for the first time and from a new perspective. I was refreshed, relieved, and happy to be alive. I realized it was the first time I felt connected to all the life around me.

I went home that evening determined to draw what I had remembered in hypnosis. I drew pictures of the entities, the ship, and a few of the tools that were used on me. When I finished, I wrote a letter to Bill. I attempted to relate all the feelings that were emerging:

> I feel relaxed and happy for the first time in years. I feel sad, too, because I know what all that stuff, submerged in my subconscious, did to me after it happened. My teenage years were a disaster. To have such a thing happen right at puberty [when] every little [normal] thing is traumatic anyway! I knew so very little back then, about my body— about sex and reproduction. I often wondered why, when I finally began having sex, at age fifteen, that I picked a partner I cared nothing about or someone I didn't even like. I felt all that stuff about the first time being special was all bullshit. I felt my virginity was something I wanted to get rid of. Knowing what I do now, I can see why. Even though it wasn't sexual and I was still physically a virgin, mentally I wasn't. That really pisses me off. That's an awful thing to do to someone. They should not have just taken me like that. Even so, I can understand them not knowing the aftereffects. For people who seem that far advanced, they sure have a lot to learn about people's feelings.
>
> So much of what I remembered was really amazing, and some of it was really beautiful. I don't want to make too many judgments from it yet. It seems too bad that the whole concept of it seems so socially unacceptable. To know something this amazing has happened in your life and not be able to say a thing to anyone for fear of being branded a lunatic...I hope it doesn't turn out to be that lonely of a thing, because I'm feeling a lot better about myself than I have in a long time.
>
> Thinking about it all today—it seems a lot like having a

baby. I know there was a hell of a lot of pain involved, but the memory of it is fading fast, while the memory of the good side of it all is getting stronger. Thank you for getting me through the hellish part of it. Even though I feel I've got more nasty little ordeals to remember, I am not afraid to tackle them.

I thought about that for a moment. I wondered what else was hiding in my subconscious. Flashes of images began to surface into my thoughts. I hoped I would be strong enough to remember without falling apart at the seams.

Even though it was the beginning of summer, I decided to visit the clearing in the woods. I would take my chances with the ticks, chiggers, and snakes. I needed to see this place where I had walked and was stolen by the visitors. I had to see if it looked like the place I had recalled in hypnosis.

Shortly after I had written the first letter to Budd Hopkins, I took a walk in the woods to retrace the steps I had taken when I had become lost. When I entered the clearing, I told myself that this was where it happened. I questioned myself at the time about what it was that had happened. I didn't know the answer.

On this second visit, I took my time looking around. I found the tree where I had first seen the little pale creatures. I walked up to the clearing, looking for anything unusual.

I found two very damaged cedar trees. Both were splayed out and twisted, as if squashed by something from above. One had been cut by the landowner. The remaining branches grew out from the base of the trunk. The other was badly damaged. Its top branches were squashed and broken. It looked as if something very large had nested in the top. Almost all the branches were damaged in some way. Some were bent around other nearby trees; some were dead, but others still grew green needles; several looked as if they had been twisted.

Whatever had happened to these trees happened years ago. I had no way of judging how long they had been damaged. I could not think of any natural phenomena that could have caused the problem. A tornado could not randomly hit one tree and twist it around another without damaging the second tree. There would have been a wide swath of destruction in the forest. I ruled out lightning. Lightning could split the limbs, but it couldn't twist them like pretzels!

I felt very calm in that area. I sat in the middle of the rocky ground at the center of the clearing. It was approximately the same spot where the beam of light had hit me. Little vegetation grew there. I didn't know if the spot was bare naturally or because of what had happened. I sat for a while and meditated on everything I had remembered about it. I felt an odd sense of security there. It was all just as I remembered in hypnosis. This time there were no small beings or huge, hovering craft, but the trees, the rocks, and the open spaces were just as I remembered. It seemed to slam the reality home. I knew there would be a lot more to remember. I could feel it inside me, waiting to surface.

I have made visits to this clearing every year since I remembered the incident in hypnosis. The tree continues to grow, although some of its limbs are dead. I recently visited the area and studied the tree closely. Its bark hangs in shreds. One limb is bent nearly in half around another tree, but unbroken and still growing green needles! It reminds me of the bent but unbroken stalks of grain in crop circles. They also continue to grow. I hope to take someone who can make a more scientific evaluation to the area with me. Every time I visit the tree, I am amazed all over again.

On my most recent visit to the tree, something unusual occurred. I circled the tree several times, looking at it. Suddenly, I became totally disoriented. I thought the clearing had disappeared! I began to panic. I had just walked out of an open spot to what I thought was the left of the tree. I didn't realize the open spot was the clearing, and I had gotten turned around in my directions. When I realized what had happened, I became very uneasy, and left the area.

I was going to have to wait a while for more hypnosis. I was ready to learn more, but Bill and his family were going on vacation for a couple of weeks. During this time, I began to lose some weight, which was wonderful. I was no longer eating due to nervous habit. I ate because I was hungry. If this was a side effect of the hypnosis, I would be tickled pink.

My sleeping habits did not change much. Some mornings I would wake up feeling exhausted, as if I had not slept at all. I had another of a series of nuclear-war dreams. (These dreams happened off and on for almost ten years.) Each time, I saw a mushroom cloud, at a distance, rising up into the sky.

Sometimes in these dreams, I would watch the fallout lightly dropping on the ground. I thought about how much it looked like snow falling. I felt such despair, knowing nothing would ever be the same again. Life, as I knew it, was over. Usually, in these dreams, I would be trudging through the streets or countryside with a group of people I didn't know. We banded together because we were all walking somewhere, looking for lost loved ones. I would wake up from these dreams very depressed. I later found out my sister had experienced similar dreams.

The dreams and the memories I was recalling had an unusual side effect. I became aware of the world around me with all its diversity of life. I began to appreciate all life forms. I was more respectful to other creatures. I no longer indiscriminately stomped on bugs or spiders. Instead, I tried to just get out of their way. I could feel my connection to all life. It was the beginning of an environmental education that continues to this day. We are all connected by the same universal life force. We are all a part of each other.

During the time Bill was gone on vacation, I tried to understand my feelings and make some sense of my life. I began to see life in much broader terms. Reality had grown from my life in my little neighborhood to the relationship I now had with a much larger universe. I began to wonder how God and Jesus fit into this greater reality.

Several months previously, I had stopped attending church. I had too many questions that were not being answered. I no longer believe in any organized religion. I still believe in God and Jesus Christ. I began to read the Bible with renewed interest. I found truths there that I had not seen before. All the stories seemed to make sense when I looked at them from a larger, universal perspective.

I began to search my inner self for right and wrong. I know when I have stepped over the boundaries of what is good behavior and what is not. I learned to trust in my own judgment. After all, churches are just the interpretations of some other human as to what God is all about. I feel my own judgment is just as good as anyone else's.

I have often said that this experience caused me to doubt most religious dogma. I mistrusted organized religion. Even so, I began to feel closer to God. I felt protected. I felt like a child taking those first, precarious steps. In essence, I lost my religion but gained my spirituality. I am open to new ideas. I would like to find a church whose theology matches my own. I am still looking.

I began to feel drawn to Native American ideas of spirituality that portray the Earth as our "mother," who should be protected. I feel we should all take care of each other. We are all connected. We are all going to sink or swim together. The looking-out-for-number-one mentality has nearly destroyed this planet. I feel we will all have to recognize the connection we have with each other in order to survive. That connection will get us through the worst of times.

Organized religion is responsible for separating humanity into small, isolated groups. Members of each group feel they are the chosen few. Their way is the only way to heaven. People should step back and look at themselves from a universal perspective.

All across the Earth, people worship a higher power. We just call it different names. If we could just see this, maybe we could see each other as part of the same family. Instead, each religion is growing into a separate faction preparing for holy wars against each other. At a time when we should be pulling together as one, we are drifting farther apart. I would love to see this change. I have an uneasy feeling it will get worse before it gets better.

The only way I know to survive is to understand myself to the best of my ability. I collect bits and pieces of all religions in my search for truth. If it feels right in my heart, I adopt the idea into my collection of Universal Truths. I trust in God to lead me in the right direction.

Chapter 5
Nightmare on Red Creek

During the hiatus between my second and third hypnosis sessions, I had an opportunity to talk to my sister about what I had learned. Sharon was one person in my family who I thought might listen objectively and understand the strangeness of this experience.

I managed to tell her all the information I had learned from my hypnosis sessions. She was very supportive. I was glad she didn't seem inclined to have me shipped off to the "funny farm." We compared a few strange experiences that had happened and wondered if any other members of the family were involved with the strange visitors. It was a relief to let someone in my family know what was happening.

That same weekend, I also told my nephew about my experiences. He related several strange incidents in his life that suggested some UFO events of his own. He and some friends had seen a strange, bright light on a camping trip and all had experienced missing time.

On July 5, 1989, I went to Bill Johnson's office for another trip down Memory Lane. Several vague memories had been bothering me, but I was not sure if I was ready to remember them fully. Bill began his relaxation techniques, and I felt myself drifting very calmly to whatever I was going to remember next.

I began to see myself driving down a road at night. (This road made me feel uneasy when I was traveling alone. One particular hilly area of it made me nervous at night.) As I crested a hill, I saw three small figures standing to the left of the road. I don't remember pulling over, but suddenly I was stopped and partly off the side of the road.

I stood outside the car. The three beings began to walk toward me. They were the same types of entities I had seen previously. (In an earlier conversation with Bill, I learned that researchers and other abductees called these creatures "grays." I began to call them grays as well, even though they looked more white than gray, in my opinion.) The grays walked across the road toward me in unison. They reminded me of the Marx Brothers walking close together with exactly the same movements. But, I wasn't laughing.

One of the beings held a wand in its hand. Tiny lightning bolts arced from its tip. The gray moved the wand around my body. I felt a strange tingling sensation—like an electric shock, but different. One of the other grays had a small box in its hands. The box had a small lens on the front. I thought I saw an image of myself reflected inside the lens.

At that point, there was a flash of light and I was inside a room. It was another exam room like the ones I had been in on other occasions. Something came up close to my right eye. It was a mechanical arm attached to a rectangular contraption. Colored lights glowed on the main body of the object, which looked computerized. A sharp point on the end of the mechanical arm was getting uncomfortably close to my eye. I felt that the point of the arm actually entered my eye, but I did not recall the experience of it under hypnosis.

The next scene that appeared to me was of myself being led toward a doorway. A different entity was with me. It was very insect-like in appearance. It looked like the grays, but the body was similar to a praying mantis. This creature urged me toward the doorway.

The door opened and a brilliant light filled the room. It reminded me of stories I had heard of near-death experiences. The light was intense and encompassing, and I could see nothing beyond it. I have often wondered what was inside that room, and if I ever entered it that night. I probably will never know.

Another gynecological examination was performed on me. A needle was inserted into my lower abdomen. It was very painful and it caused my stomach to cramp. After this procedure, I was returned to my car. I could not recall when this experience occurred, and I did not remember if I had noticed any missing time.

As we finished this episode, Bill asked me if I would like to explore any other memories. I began to remember something that had happened one night in the fall of 1980. I was on a date with a fellow I will call "Rob." We had only known each other for a few weeks at this time, but I was infatuated with him. We drove out to a dirt road near Red Creek in southern Mississippi. We drove a while before we stopped on the road to "park and spark."

My conscious memory was of parking on this deserted road. While watching the stars, we saw an unusual light in the sky. Later we had sex in the car and then drove home. The strangest part of this memory was of having sex with Rob, but during the experience he seemed to change into someone else. It left me feeling very strange.

The memory I recalled in hypnosis was very different. As Bill regressed me further, I remembered that Rob and I got out of the car and sat on the hood to watch the stars. I saw what looked like a satellite moving across the sky, and I mentioned this to Rob. We watched it move across the sky. As it traveled overhead, it stopped. It began to move again, but in the opposite direction. I didn't think satellites could do that! It stopped again and began to move back in the direction of its original course.

I said, "Did you see that? Tell me what you saw!"

Rob described movement identical to what I had seen. We talked a short while about UFOs and the possibilities of what was out there in the universe. I began to feel a fear rising in me. I looked at all the trees surrounding us on that dirt road. I felt that we were being watched, and I felt very vulnerable.

I didn't mention the fear I was feeling to Rob. I told him I was cold because the fear had caused me to shiver. We got off the hood of the car to get inside, where it was warmer. Suddenly there was a whooshing sound, and, on the dirt road in front of us, a bell-shaped craft appeared! I looked at Rob and he just stood there, not moving. There was a blank expression on his face, and he was completely motionless. It was as if he had been shut off like a light switch.

From the bottom of the craft dropped three bluish-white rings of light. A couple of grays came down through the rings and began to walk toward me. I began to panic. I screamed at Rob, "Don't let them take me!"

He just stood there as if he were in a trance. The grays came up to me and took me by the arms. They started to lead me to the craft until I was underneath it. I felt that I was being sucked up inside of the thing.

Everything was dark inside, so I could not see very well. I felt the familiar screen come up hiding the memory of what happened. I was blocking it. I didn't want to remember. Bill tried a different tactic by asking me how I felt after I left the ship.

"I felt cold," I said. "Something's wrong!"

Bill asked me, "What did they do?"

Images began to flash before my eyes. I didn't like what I saw, and I could not say what I was seeing. I could only moan, "Nooooo!"

I was crying and extremely upset. I was on a table, but this time it was not for an exam. I told Bill a creature was with me. He was different from the others I had seen; he seemed to be part gray and part human.

I didn't want to remember, but I could not hide from the image any longer. This creature came up to me as I lay naked on the table. The table moved and my legs were forced apart. The creature entered me and I screamed. This was something I had never heard about in any other abduction reports, and it was horrifying. The half-gray was skinny and almost insect-like in appearance. His penis was long and thin; he was not able to get all of it inside me. I could not move to get away. It was a very clinical rape.

When the creature ejaculated, I felt drenched with its semen. It burned and irritated me both inside and outside my vagina. I felt like I was in shock. The room was dimly lit, but I could see other grays standing and watching. I could sense they were pleased with this creature's performance. It seemed to be a test to see if this creature was functional. I cannot put into words how much I hated them at that moment. I had never felt that much anger in my life. I couldn't remember anything else after that, although I believe they took a small tissue sample from my right buttock.

When I was returned, Rob was still standing there. A short time later, he regained consciousness. The ship was gone, and my memory of what had just happened was gone. I felt awful and cold. Rob and I left a short time later.

I don't know if Rob and I actually had sex that night or not. I doubt it. I feel that was a screen memory to cover up what had actually happened. I don't know if they did anything to Rob while I was gone. He does not have any memory of any of this occurring, except for the original sighting of the strangely moving satellite.

Bill brought me out of hypnosis. I had remembered a lot for one night, and I felt completely drained emotionally. I was numb. Bill began to reassure me that it was not my fault and I had a right to be angry. He told me all the things you would tell a rape victim, but this was no ordinary rape. This thing wasn't even human!

I had to find a way to sort through all the anger I was feeling. I began to wonder what kind of nightmare life I was living. How could I have kept a memory like that suppressed? Would it happen again? The 40-mile drive home was a long one that night. I knew, now, why I was afraid of the dark.

Chapter 6
Rage

I awoke the next morning feeling soiled from the experience I had remembered. I was still angry, too. I hated how I felt, and I wasn't sure what to do about it. I wondered if I had made a mistake by digging into this whole UFO business. These aliens now seemed less benevolent than I had originally thought. I wondered if even worse memories were hidden in my subconscious.

I cursed the creatures that had disrupted my life. I called them every disgusting name I could think of. I knew my opinions did not matter to them, but it made me feel a little better. My ranting was probably as insignificant as the buzzing of a captured insect. It was the only release I had available to me. After I had exhausted my expletives, I decided to write another letter to Bill Johnson. I tried to convey the emotions that were running through me:

Dear Bill,
        What kind of life am I living, anyway? How many

more of my memories are just cover-up stories for these nasty little liaisons? Is my life my own, or do I belong to them? Have my choices and decisions been influenced by them?

I alternate between feelings of extreme anger and disgust. I do mean extreme! I have never felt (consciously) such an intense feeling of hate and rage. It's scary and I don't know how to deal with it. I can feel it boiling away inside and there's nowhere to direct it—to let it out. I don't want to punch the wall, or kick my dog, or explode at some poor person who just happens to piss me off at the wrong moment. The ones I need to unload on are long gone. I think one of the things that pissed me off the most was the fact that it was such a devastating thing for me, and the bug-eyed ones were standing there, watching in approval. I felt that. They were pleased by what was happening! I do have the impression that this was that creature's first attempt to have sex with one of us. That's why the big-eyes were so pleased. I feel that it was a clinical rape. That's what it felt like. There was no malice toward me, just an incredible, overwhelming insensitivity. I probably would have felt similar had I been raped by a dog or other animal. I suspect it was one of the "half-n-halfs." He was taller than the others and had strange eyes. I felt he was pretty young. How young, I'm not sure, but compared to the others, he was younger.

Now for the sex organs (ick!): his penis was skinny in proportion to the length. It seemed unusually pale—almost white (ick! ick! ick!). I noticed no pubic hair, and I don't know about testicles. If he had any, I think they were up close to his body and not hanging loose. When that thing orgasmed, or ejaculated, or whatever it is they do, I felt he drenched me in this stuff (sicko!). There was a whole lot of fluid and it irritated my vagina. I think it irritated the tissues or something.

I felt so bizarre describing the sex organ of an extraterrestrial! This was ideal fodder for the tabloids. I could see it now: "Earth Girls Are Easy! Hometown Girl Involved In Alien Tryst!" Except this was not fun and games. It was horrific and painful. The hardest part was not being able to tell anyone what was happening to me. I was able to tell Nadine, but it was difficult. It all sounded so perverse! I needed to talk, but I did not want to admit that I had had sex with an alien.

My physical condition improved after this particular hypnosis session. The week before I had had numerous headaches. These disappeared after I remembered what had occurred. It was as if the memory was festering inside me and had to come out. I did not want to remember, but it could no longer stay hidden. It was time to know. It was a relief to release the memory. It was not pleasant, but it was necessary.

I felt that this had to be one of the most traumatic things that had ever happened to me. I had remembered, and it did not kill me. I survived and felt stronger. I began to see a strength in me that I had not realized was there. I had always felt I was a weak person. I had a poor self image. I always thought I was like a rabbit scared of its own shadow.

Now I realized that I had survived the unimaginable, absorbed the experience into my subconscious, and continued on with my life. No one knew, not even me. The horror of it should have put me in a catatonic state. It was that bad. How did I survive this experience? I don't understand the workings of the mind, but it seems to have a great self-protection mode. It buries the trauma until the conscious mind is able to accept and deal with the aftermath.

I have been asked if the experience changed my ability to have a normal sex life. That's a good question. A normal response might be a total aversion to sex after such a traumatic episode. I never had that type of response. I just absorbed the experience and pushed it into some dark corner of my subconscious. If anything, the experience made me appreciate the warmth of human sexuality.

As the days progressed, I remembered other possible incidents that had occurred in my life. It seemed that each recalled memory triggered others to come to mind. How many more? It seemed my whole life was turning into one big screen memory. I had lived a double life that I was not even aware of on a conscious level. It was very disturbing.

It began to change my whole conception of consciousness and reality. I began to think with a broader vision. I began to hunger for knowledge. I felt I was emerging from isolation and wanted to know everything about the world around me.

After each hypnosis session, I would have flashes of memory that sparked new curiosity. It was as if I were being allowed to remember events in a specific order. It was not chronological. I would jump around from one age to another. As I gained strength of mind, more recollections were available to me. I had to be strong enough to deal with the memories. I believe everything emerged when I was mentally strong enough to cope with it.

The next area I was to explore concerned an incident at the high school I attended. Something very strange happened one night at a school slumber party. I had a very conscious memory of an experience that night. I was nervous about remembering it. I was not sure if it was an extraterrestrial or a supernatural event. I was also curious because this experience occurred in a room adjoining a gymnasium filled with wide-awake, noisy, teenaged girls. I didn't know what to expect, but I knew that exploring this experience was the next step in learning what was happening to me.

Chapter 7
Rainbow

For this next hypnosis session, Bill brought an assistant to help with questions, notes, and observation. Jean Brogan is a small woman with a big sense of humor. Even though I was nervous about a new person knowing my strange secrets, I liked her immediately. She was a clinical social worker. We talked a little while longer, then settled into the session.

I began to make myself comfortable on my foam mat. I found that I was becoming used to the process of hypnosis. I knew what to expect and was able to respond to the relaxation techniques. I knew which incident I wanted to explore. As Bill moved me through the relaxation techniques, I began to see the high school that I attended as a youth.

On that night, long ago, I arrived at the gymnasium for a slumber party. I was a member of a girl's club that sponsored the annual event. About fifty girls brought blankets, radios, food, and other necessary items to the gym that night—everything we needed to keep us well-fed and entertained.

As the evening progressed, a small group of friends gathered in the gym's lobby. It was a quiet place away from the rest of the noisy females. We sat and gossiped and told each other spooky stories. We had a curious interest in the supernatural, and the darkened lobby provided a good backdrop for strange tales. We decided to try an experimental seance. It seemed like an adventurous thing to do. I don't believe any of us knew what we were getting into.

Mrs. Green (pseudonym), our teacher and sponsor for the evening, came into the lobby. She was young and had a good rapport with all of us. We told her what we were planning. She seemed interested in what we were doing and decided to watch. This reinforced our opinion that she was a "cool teacher."

We sat in a circle and held hands as we began the seance. We tried to contact the spirit of Jimi Hendrix, a rock musician who had recently died of a drug overdose. Our efforts were fruitless. Undaunted, we decided to try someone else. One of the girls in our circle suggested we try to contact a recently deceased relative. We all agreed, and once again attempted to reach the spirits.

I don't know how much time passed before I saw a white, transparent cloud enter the lobby through a window. It stayed at ceiling level until it reached our small circle.

Suddenly I felt enveloped in whiteness. I fought for breath. I felt pinned against the wall by some intense force. I could not see anything at first. The outside door to the gym was opened and six small figures entered the lobby. I and four of the other females were selected from the group. The remaining girls were "shut off." They seemed unaware of what was happening.

The five of us were led, zombie-like, out the door and into the night. Above the field next to the school was a huge, circular craft. It was saucer-shaped and had a row of colored lights underneath. I could not believe that such a thing could be there without being noticed, as several houses stood nearby and it was only about 11 PM.

Once we were underneath the object, we each floated up into the bottom of it. I noticed that one of my friends was crying, but I heard no sound.

As I entered the craft, I lost track of the others. I was led down a narrow hallway. I remember feeling upset and guilty. I felt it was my fault that the others were involved. I blamed myself for whatever was happening to them. It was an irrational thought, but I felt I had led them into this situation.

The small visitor who led me down the hall looked the same as the creatures in my previous experiences. It was pale and fragile-looking with large, black eyes. It was one of the grays. The name seems to fit their lack of personalities rather than their skin color.

We entered a room, and I was brought in front of an entity of a different sort. This creature was tall and very slender with very long arms and legs. It looked somewhat like a huge walking stick or praying mantis. Its head contained dark eyes like the others, but its jaw seemed to be extended out from its face. This creature looked at me in a curious way. I felt as if I were being paraded in front of it for some unknown reason. There was an air of authority about the creature that was intimidating. I think it said something to me, but I do not remember what. I think it told me not to be afraid—that I wouldn't be hurt.

I was escorted out of that room and into another. I was stripped of my clothing and placed on a table. Several of the small grays were in the room. One came near and looked at me very closely. One of the beings brought over a tube with a needle attached. It inserted the needle into my abdomen, just above my hip bone. A dark, emerald-green fluid in the tube seemed to bubble slightly during the procedure. I felt a dull, cramping ache in my belly.

Then I had my clothes back on and was being taken to another room. The room was dimly lit and empty, except for a small lighted cubicle. I was led up to this object. I looked inside. It was a baby! It was a strange, sickly-looking infant that seemed to be part human and part gray. It was frightening and fascinating.

The child looked up at me from its bed. Its eyes contained whites and irises, but they were much larger than normal. It had a small, delicate nose and mouth, and its head seemed oversized compared to its body. Its skin was almost transparent. It reminded me of a baby bird that I had found when I was younger. I could almost see its internal organs through its skin.

The grays who were with me told me to pick the child up and hold it. They indicated to me that this child was mine. It had been conceived a year earlier during one of their visits. I was startled by this information and denied that I could have given birth to such a thing. It scared me; I didn't want to look at it. I surely did not want to touch it! The grays were insistent.

With reluctance, I picked up the child-thing. She was as light as a feather. As soon as I held her in my arms, I knew she was female, and I knew she was mine. There was something telepathic that passed between us. I just knew I was her mother. She looked intently into my face, and I smiled at her. She was not nearly as ugly as I first thought. I looked at all her tiny little features. She seemed to be about six months old, but it was difficult to tell for sure.

The grays watched the interaction between us. Telepathically they indicated I should try to nurse her. This confused me at first, but I realized they wanted me to breast-feed her. I lifted up my shirt and awkwardly brought the baby up to my breast. The little one seemed to be as confused as I was about what to do.

The grays appeared to be somewhat disappointed that I was not able to nurse her. I held her close to me and thought, "I'm gonna name you 'Rainbow.'" I felt I already loved this little one. She made a little squeak of a sound in response to my thought. I wanted to take her home with me. The grays approached me and started to take her away from me.

"No! She's mine!" I cried. " I want to keep her!"

The beings told me I could not take her with me. They said she had to stay with them. They took her and placed her back in the bed cubicle. This was so unfair to me! I felt they should not have showed her to me at all if they were going to take her away. I began to cry as they led me from the room.

I was brought to an area where my friends stood. One by one, we were dropped out of the ship. It was like being lowered in a swift-moving, invisible elevator. We trailed across the parking lot back into the gym. Each of us moved back to the places where we had been sitting.

At that moment, I felt the white light pinning me up against the wall again. Then, suddenly, the light was gone and the pressure was released. It was as if someone had flipped a switch and it was gone. It seemed as if we were all released at once.

Instantly we all panicked and screamed. A couple of the girls were hysterical. Mrs. Green was frantic! She had condoned the seance, and suddenly we were all out of control. I ran into the main body of the gym with several others. We yanked open the swinging doors that separated us from the crowd of girls on the gym floor.

We blubbered to some of our other friends, telling them what had happened to us. They all were rather uninterested. I had already forgotten everything except the white cloud and being slammed up against the wall. These seemed to be what most of us remembered. A couple of the girls said they had felt someone touch them on the shoulder.

Bill asked me if I remembered being visited a year earlier. I described a brief encounter in which the grays entered my room and did a quick procedure similar to the one I had just recalled. A needle was poked into my abdomen, and something was removed. The entities left soon afterward. This must have been when the child was conceived.

Bill began to bring me out of hypnosis. It had been another long, eventful evening. I opened my eyes groggily. Jean and Bill and I discussed the night's information.

I began to think of everything I had just witnessed. A child! I felt angry that they had stolen her from me. This seemed so unfair! I thought of her as I drove home that night. Tiny little Rainbow. I hope she is okay. Even though she looked different, she was still my child. I wondered how much she knew about me. How could she know I cared?

Chapter 8
Davy Jones's Locker

The incident at the school left me with many unanswered questions. I could not understand how something like this could happen in the middle of our small town. How could these creatures come into a gymnasium full of noisy females and take us with no one noticing? The craft was in plain sight of a row of homes, but no one looked out the windows that I could see. I was looking for some sign of life, and there was none. Our small group walked out of the school and rose up into the spacecraft unnoticed.

I was concerned about my other friends, whom I had seen go aboard the craft. I had not seen several of them in more than 15 years. I could not remember some of the girls who were in the circle. I knew those I spent time with back then, but I could not definitely name all who sat in on that seance. I have since spoken to several of my friends who were in the circle that night. We all know something strange occurred, but, so far, no one wants to dig into what happened. I will not say whom I saw go into the craft with me. I can only say that some were taken and some were shut off.

Bill performed several hypnosis sessions in the weeks that followed. Most revealed repeats of the procedure of egg extraction. I would be placed on a table, and a type of needle or tube would be stuck into my lower abdomen. I appear to have undergone this procedure many times. I don't know how many times.

During the first week of August, I decided to dig into an episode that had been bothering me. I had a conscious memory of contact with someone who claimed to work for the government. I had a pretty substantial recollection of this encounter, but I felt there was more information that I could not remember.

My conscious memory left me confused and full of questions. In late 1980 or early 1981, I was working as a waitress in a seafood restaurant/bar near the harbor on the Gulf Coast. The place served a wide array of customers. Lawyers and bankers from downtown regularly came in for cocktails and dinner. But the restaurant was next to the harbor, and sailors of all nationalities stopped in to eat and drink. It made for some very interesting evenings, and it was quite a fun place to work.

After several months of working at this restaurant, I got to know the "regulars." On some nights after my shift ended, I would sit at the bar and have a few drinks before going home.

One night I was talking to a man I will call "Ben." He ran a charter fishing boat in the harbor. Ben said if I would give him a ride to his boat, he would give me a tour. He was very proud of his boat.

I had visited with Ben on many occasions, and I felt comfortable enough to leave with him. I parked the car in front of the many boats docked in the marina. Ben led me to the slip where his boat was moored. It was an average 30-foot fishing boat with a small cabin. Ben grabbed a couple of beers from the cooler and led me up a ladder to where the captain's chairs were located.

We had not been sitting there very long when two people arrived. I only remember them as being male and female. Ben went out to meet them, and they talked for a while. Ben introduced me to the two, and then I went back up to the captain's seat because Ben needed to speak privately with his friends.

He returned after the two people left. He had what I assumed to be a marijuana cigarette in his hand. I used to smoke pot often in earlier years. Since the birth of my daughter, I did not feel comfortable stoned. It was as if my body chemistry changed, and the effect was different. Old habits die hard, however. When Ben lit the joint, I took a hit.

Things got strange after that. I took one or two hits, but never saw Ben take one. The next thing I remember was looking at the stars from the window in front of me. I no longer saw the lights of the harbor.

Ben began to tell me of some of his Navy experiences. He mentioned being in a special forces-type group. It was a very elite bunch. He told me of a secret-government base that was located underwater.

He said, "We wore orange jumpsuit uniforms like the guys in the movie *Close Encounters*." He was referring to the group of humans that were chosen to board the spacecraft near the end of the movie. I was amazed at what he was telling me. I felt very strange and attributed my feeling to being under the influence of marijuana.

Ben told me that boats would take them out on the water. There were pilings out in the sea where the boats would dock. He told me submarines would meet them and take them down to a base.

It was then that I began to feel very odd and uneasy. I remember thinking a question, "Are you an alien?" I have no idea why this question came to mind. I did not know of my involvement at that time. To my surprise, even though I had not voiced my query, Ben answered me.

He said, "No, but I work with them."

I began to feel very strange and uncomfortable. I was beginning to remember something that I was not prepared to understand. Ben looked at me and said, "You do know what is happening with you, don't you?"

I really had no idea, but I heard myself say, "Yes."

He saw my discomfort and said, "Yeah, it's really hard when you first find out. It gets easier."

I could not believe this conversation we were having! It was becoming too strange. Ben said, "I still have connections with this group. I can arrange for you to go there." He was referring to the underwater base. "There are things there that you couldn't begin to imagine! The only condition is you, basically, have to drop off the face of the earth. You can't tell family or anyone that you are going."

I really wanted to go! It seemed like such an exciting opportunity. I thought of my baby daughter and knew I could not abandon her. I told Ben, "I want to go, but I have a baby now. I just can't leave her. I wish you'd asked me sooner, but I can't. I can't do that to my family."

He seemed irritated with my response. He said, "This is the only time I'll ask. This is your only chance to go."

I felt as if I were letting a great adventure slip through my fingers, but I told him I could not go now. I began to feel very nervous about this conversation. My memories about what happened next are incomplete.

I remember saying, "I really have to go now!"

I was feeling scared. I think a lifetime of memories were beginning to surface, and I was not ready to face them. I remember rising to leave. I leaned over and gave Ben a kiss on the cheek as I was leaving. He gave me a really strange look—as if he did not know what to think about me.

I walked out to the car and got in. I sat there for nearly 20 minutes, thinking, "Did we really talk about what I think we talked about?" Already the memory of it was beginning to disappear. I felt as if I had been in some altered state that went way beyond just being stoned.

I only saw Ben one time in the restaurant after that night. He had been quite a regular until that time. He came in and sat at the bar. We said hello and nothing else. He left soon after, and I never saw him again.

The hypnosis session that focused on this incident yielded very little new information. Essentially everything was conscious recall. I did get a few extra details. The underwater base was called the Poseidon Complex, but it was more affectionately known as Davy Jones's Locker. I feel that Ben and I talked about much more that has been erased from my memory.

I recently attempted another hypnosis session focused on the same incident. Still no hidden secrets emerged. I have come to the conclusion that some sort of drug may have been laced into that joint I smoked. I must have been taken out to sea or somewhere. That would explain why some of the time I saw stars out the window, while at other times I saw the harbor lights.

I still have questions about this incident. How did this guy know about me before *I* knew about me? I did not begin to suspect I was an abductee until 1987. How did Ben know seven years earlier? Am I on somebody's Big List somewhere? Why was I given the choice to go to this government base? He could have easily taken me there against my will.

The last time I was on the Gulf, I drove down to the harbor. The boat is still there. I looked in the telephone book, and Ben is still the captain and still runs a charter fishing business. I have tried to gather my nerve to go talk to him. I doubt if he would admit to anything he told me unless we were alone. I don't think I would want to be alone with him and tell him I remember everything. Sometimes I wish I could confront him and tell him I am ready to go now. Maybe I would find the answers I am searching for. I just do not want to disappear.

Chapter 9
Communication Breakthrough

In August 1989, my world was changing rapidly. I was trying to fit all I was learning into the life I had to live. I looked at all the people living their lives and I envied their "normalcy." My life had never been normal—and now I finally understood why. I looked at my coworkers and friends and wondered. What would they think if I told them my story? Would they still be my friends? I was thankful that I had Nadine to confide in. I told her of everything that came out in hypnosis, no matter how strange. I didn't realize my life would get even more bizarre.

I decided to focus a hypnosis session on the strange image I recalled just after I had met Bill Johnson. It was a memory of a creature with what appeared to be sharp teeth. It was in a darkened room that was vaguely familiar to me. I knew this creature was not a typical "gray." It was different and more frightening.

During this hypnosis session, I recalled an incident that had occurred when I was a six-year-old child:

I was playing in my backyard one day and decided to go inside my father's work shed. I had often been warned not to play in this shed because it contained a lot of tools, nails, and objects that could cause injury to a young child. Also, it was my father's territory and he didn't want children playing there and losing his tools. Knowing this was a forbidden zone made it all the more appealing.

I cautiously walked into the shed and stood still while my eyes adjusted to the darkness of the shed's interior. The building smelled of moldy, decaying wood. It was old and not insulated or protected from the weather. Parts of the roof leaked, causing mildew.

As my eyes grew accustomed to the light, I realized I was not alone! A strange creature stood upright on the opposite side of the building. This entity looked like a small dinosaur—a miniature version of a Tyrannosaurus Rex that I had seen on TV. It had very functional, muscular arms. It was holding a small piece of a motor that belonged to my father and was looking at it as if trying to figure out how it worked.

Just as I realized what I was seeing, the creature turned to look at me. The coldness of the stare of this oversized reptile frightened me. Its head movement was quick—almost bird-like. Its face was smaller and more tapered than that of a tyranosaur, and its mouth was smaller. It looked as if it contained sharp teeth, but it might have been some sort of mask or breathing apparatus.

Its eyes reminded me of a cat's or a snake's eyes. They were a dark, brownish-orange with slit pupils. A bony ridge ran from between its eyes, over the top of its head, and down the back of its neck and spine. Raised, rib-like structures fanned out from another bony ridge along the center of its chest. I could not recall what the entity looked like from the chest down.

The reptilian looked at me and began to move toward me. I was very frightened. I couldn't make a sound to scream. I backed up against the wall behind me as the creature moved closer. It seemed to be about five feet tall (several feet taller than I was). It moved uncomfortably close to me and looked me over. I felt very threatened by the thing. I lost control of my bladder and wet my pants.

I could not "read" any thoughts from this reptilian, but a disconcerting feeling radiated from the creature. (Now, as an adult, I recognize the feeling. The thing was lecherous.) I didn't know what was going to happen, but I sensed great danger.

Just as the reptilian bent slightly to look at me more closely, a gray entity was suddenly there with us! It reached out and touched the reptile's arm. The creature backed away from me. I sensed it was irritated with the gray and there seemed to be some connection between the two. It was as if the gray told it to leave me alone and the reptilian obeyed reluctantly.

I don't remember what happened after that. I was glad to be out of that situation. I don't understand the meaning of the incident, and I don't know why the gray appeared to "save" me. It may have been a form of the "good cop, bad cop routine." Perhaps this was only an act to manipulate me into feeling protected by the grays. I may never know. The reptilian seemed to be lower in the hierarchy of these visitors. The big, muscular creature could easily have overpowered the gray physically, but it backed off with just a touch from the gray, as if an unspoken communication had passed between them.

I now had a new entity to face. I hoped never to see this reptilian type again. It seemed primitive, powerful, dangerous, and cold-blooded. I have often wondered if it was some sort of evolved dinosaur. Could some dinosaurs have been saved from destruction by a race who have visited Earth for millions of years? I added this to my growing list of speculative thoughts.

The experiences I was having seemed to get more and more complex. New creatures and new fears were emerging, and I had more questions than answers. I did not suspect that I was soon to receive answers to some of my questions from a new and unknown source. I did not think my life could get any stranger, but, once again, I was wrong.

My first telepathic communication came early one morning while I was preparing for a National Guard weekend duty. I was drinking coffee and thinking of all I had learned. I thought of Rainbow and all the times I had remembered the egg-extraction exams. I thought to myself, "I wonder how many more babies I have that I don't know about?"

Suddenly, an answer popped into my head. It felt like my own thoughts but appeared conversational. It said, "*You have twenty children.*"

I thought, "BULLSHIT!"

The "Voice" continued, "*Eighteen are with us.*"

I decided to play along with it. "How many boys and how many girls?"

The Voice said, "*Eleven girls and nine boys.*"

This was spooky! I thought, "Boy, I am really losing it now!" I had always heard that you should not worry when you talk to yourself. Only when you answer yourself should you begin to worry! Was I answering, or was it someone else? It had the same feel as my own thoughts, but it did not feel like me. The answers came too quickly. The numbers of 11 and 9 came faster than I would have been able to put together.

I thought of more questions to ask during my 90-minute drive to the armory. And each time I had a few moments of spare time, I would write down the answers to my questions. It became a running conversation that went like this:

Jeanne: "Who is the father of these children?"

Voice: "*There are many fathers who watch over them.*"

Jeanne: "Who is the biological father? Who gave up the seed to make them?"

Voice: "*I did.*"

Jeanne: "Who are you?"

Voice: "*Queetzal.*"

I was surprised to hear a name. And the name sounded like a name a sixties rock star might give his child.

Queetzal: (Referring to a drawing of mine) "*The bird is a*

phoenix. It symbolizes the rebirth of our species. We were a dying race, until we began breeding with your people."

Jeanne: "Doesn't that sort of dilute the species?"

Queetzal: *"It is better to be diluted than nonexistent."*

Jeanne: "What are you, anyway?"

Queetzal: *"I am the one, like the picture you drew. We are called by many names, but you may call us Reeg-o-lays."*

This was sounding ludicrous. Were they named after a salad dressing or a corn chip?!

Jeanne: "How about the other kind? Like the one with the long arms and legs?"

Queetzal: *"That was Zan-o-pria. She is the eldest of the Trilobites."*

(I know how stupid it sounds! I am relaying the information as it was given to me.)

Jeanne: "She is similar to you?"

Queetzal: *"Same species, different race. [Beings of] her type are very rare. Similar to the queen of bees on your planet. She is very old and respected."*

Jeanne: "Are you old?"

Queetzal: *"Yes, we have a long life span."*

Jeanne: "How old?"

Queetzal: "*Age is irrelevant.*"

I realized I was carrying on quite a conversation. I decided to take advantage of the opportunity to ask questions.

Jeanne: "Who is God?"

Queetzal: "*God is the infinite power of the universe. Every living thing in the universe is connected by the force of life. This combined life force creates a power higher than any of its individual parts.*"

This was really getting deep. Where were my hip boots when I needed them? I expected him to say "May the force be with you" next!

Jeanne: "What is the devil?"

Queetzal: "*It is choosing to do what you know is wrong.*"

Jeanne: "What is hell?"

Queetzal: "*Infinite, unchangeable regret.*"

I wondered what my fellow soldiers would think if they knew what I was doing. I began to feel uneasy about being military. I had a secret clearance because my MOS (Military Occupational Specialty) required it. And I was conversing with aliens in my thoughts. This was not good.

I began to think of the impulsive urge that had driven me to enter the military. The idea just popped into my head one day in 1985. A week later I was sworn in and property of the US Army. It did not seem nearly as strange as it does now. I was 30 years old then and had a five-year-old and a 20-month-old toddler! Yet, I felt it was something I had to do. Thus began my short career as "Combat Mommy."

I served two years in the Regular Army. I enjoyed military life to some degree. I might still be in the Army today had I not been sexually harassed by several fellow soldiers. They made my life miserable until I wanted nothing more than to be back home. After my discharge, I joined the National Guard. I enjoyed it. It was a kinder and gentler situation. We still performed our duties but maintained our souls! I enjoyed the two week training duty that I had to attend every year. I was able to visit new places and still have a home life. The weekend duties were sometimes tedious, but it was a necessary tedium.

Upon returning from my weekend duty, I sent Bill all the information the thought voice had given me. Bill told me to keep writing everything down. He assured me I was okay and urged me to keep him informed if anything else happened.

Several days later, I felt a strong urge to grab a pen and paper. It was a strange feeling that would become very familiar to me. I began to receive information on many different subjects. Queetzal would tell me why they were doing things to me and would give me spiritual advice and ecological warnings.

That urgent feeling would hit me, and I would grab a pen and write on anything I could find. If I was busy, the information would still come into my head. I would try to remember what I was told so I could write it down when I could get to it. Often I would lose the information if I did not write it down as I received it. It would just be gone.

I lost some very descriptive (and possibly important) details because I just was not able to write down information immediately. Losing the information frustrated me. I felt guilty for not being able to write it down. I usually felt drained and tired after writing. If it was possible, I would lie down and rest for a few minutes.

One day in the latter part of 1989, I was given some new information. I was supposed to be at the Pyramid of the Sun in Teotihuacan, Mexico, at the time of the vernal equinox of 1996. I felt that something significant was supposed to happen at that time. I was not sure if this was the Big Exodus for another world, but that was the impression I felt. How was I supposed to get there? Why couldn't they pick me up here? I had many unanswered questions.

I wrote to Bill about this message. I told him that I thought it was interesting, but I could not take it seriously. I was not going to be found on top of a pyramid with my children and dog and American Traveler luggage, waiting for the Great Pumpkin to arrive! I filed this information away with the rest. As I write this, that date has come and gone. I spent the whole day serving tourists in the restaurant where I was employed. I was too busy to think about what was happening at the pyramid, and I have not heard if anything ever did. And unfortunately, no one "beamed me up" that day to relieve me from my job at the restaurant.

The more information I received, the more fascinated I became with it. The writings began to come to me on a regular basis. I collected the information and stored it in various places. I could carry on conversations or watch TV and still write whatever needed to be written. I did not "trance out" and lose awareness of what was happening around me. It remains to this day one of the most unusual aspects of my ongoing experiences.

Chapter 10
The Crystal City

In the fall of 1989, I began taking some classes at a local college. I found I had an insatiable thirst for learning. I wanted to know everything. I was also getting tutored by "The Voice" that was with me so much of the time. While I listened to class lectures on religion or science, "Queetz" made comment after comment in my mind. Sometimes he disagreed with the teacher and told me why. Sometimes he stressed the importance of learning and knowing the information I was being given.

It was around this time that I began to be drawn to books on many different subjects. I could go into a library and scan the shelves, and a book would catch my attention. Each time this happened, the book contained something that I felt was important to learn. Sometimes it was only a paragraph or a sentence, but I would know when I found it.

One book that I was drawn to was Louis Lamour's, *The Haunted Mesa*. I had never read any of his books before, nor have I read any since. I enjoy Western movies, but Western books seldom interested me. I began to read this one. To my surprise, the story was about a tribe of Native Americans who knew about a window to another dimension. This tribe would pass through the window to a different world. I was blown away! What was I being shown here? Why? I just absorbed all the information and mentally filed it under Infinite Possibilities. That file has now grown quite large!

As time went on, my memories continued to surface in a seemingly random fashion. It was as if I was allowed to remember certain events when I became strong enough to deal with the memories emotionally. Memories would trigger other memories that I felt I needed to explore.

I had a feeling about an incident that had occurred in 1985, while traveling from Mississippi to Missouri with my two children. It happened as I drove through a remote area of northern Arkansas, near the last leg of the journey. I decided to drive this route because I could stay on the Interstate highway for 40 more miles and make better time.

I exited the Interstate onto scenic Route 7. It was a steep and curvy two-lane highway that afforded a wonderful view of the Ozark Mountains. It was late evening-too dark to enjoy any of the scenery I was passing through. I remember feeling very anxious as I drove along the highest elevation of that stretch of road. I encountered no traffic. I started feeling very vulnerable driving alone with my two youngsters.

I looked up at the stars through my front windshield as I was driving. I think I pulled off the road onto a scenic overlook. I know this road trip was longer than it should have been. Normally I could drive that distance in 11 or 12 hours, but this trip lasted more than 13 hours. I felt that something may have happened when I stopped at the overlook.

I met with Bill and Jean for another hypnosis session in order to explore my memories of this trip. Bill regressed me to when I had pulled into the overlook. I recalled turning off the car engine and stepping out of the car. I began to hear a low humming sound. The sound grew louder. As I stood there, a disk-shaped craft rose out of the valley to my right. It ascended to a height of about 15 feet. A ramp dropped out of the bottom of the craft, and several small grays seemed to float down it toward my car.

I looked at my children who were still in the car. My daughter was watching, but my son was still asleep in his car seat.

The beings began to walk, stiff-legged, like toy soldiers, toward us. Two of the grays came to me, and two walked over to my daughter. They escorted us to the craft.

I became upset about leaving my 20-month-old son alone in the car. A thought/voice told me, "*It will be okay.*"

I watched my daughter move up the ramp as if she were on an escalator. I followed soon after. I felt a strange floating sensation as I moved up into the ship.

Once I was inside, I could not see my daughter anywhere. I was upset. I yelled, "Don't hurt her!" Once again, a voice in my head calmed me. "She will be okay," it said.

I was led into a brightly lit room. A bench-like object projected from the wall. A small gray approached me with a vial of yellowish-brown liquid in its hand. A thought/voice said, "Why don't you drink this?"

I balked at the idea of ingesting this unknown substance. It could be poison for all I knew.

The voice said, "Take it and feel this. It will help you understand."

Without thinking or protesting, I took the vial and swallowed the liquid. It was very bitter, and I felt like I was going to vomit. The visitors watched me for a moment. I began to feel dizzy and light-headed. The grays took me over to the bench and I sat down.

All my surroundings began to fade out. Suddenly, I was observing a beach scene from the air. It looked familiar to me and seemed like a calm and peaceful place. Everything seemed to be tinted orange, like a sunset. Everything was tinted that way—the sky, the rocks, and the beach.

I noticed someone walking alone on the sand. The beach had large rocks on it that obscured my view of what lay ahead. I was reminded of the Pacific coast in Oregon. I moved to a different position and was able to get a better view of the walker. She was a hybrid mix, but she looked more human than alien. She had abnormally large eyes and wispy blond hair.

This young girl did not seem to be aware of me as she walked along. As we passed by some of the larger rocks, I was able to see farther down the beach. What I saw took my breath away! Nestled in the rocky cove was a glass-like structure. It was a large area that looked to be part of an enclosed dwelling built into the rocks. It was incredibly beautiful!

The shape of this structure reminded me of the Aztec or Mayan pyramids. The glass was translucent and iridescent with many colors sparkling in the sun. It looked as if it were made of pinkish opal. I was awed by the sight of such beauty. This was one fine condo on the beach! It reminded me of the description of Heaven in the Bible—a city of jewels.

The girl walked toward the buildings. As I followed her, a thought came into my head, "This is one of the New Cities." I suddenly became aware that the girl was my child, Rainbow! I don't know how I knew, but I knew! She seemed to be in her teens, but I could not be sure. She looked smaller than a human of similar age.

She entered an arched doorway. I followed her in. Inside the structure was a park or garden area. Plaster or marble columns and walls were covered with an ivy made of round, blue leaves. It coated the top of the wall like a carpet. The wall seemed to be about six feet tall and surrounded the entire park.

In the center of the park was a columned gazebo area. Around the outside of the gazebo were strange plants with red, star-like flowers. The sky was pinkish-purple. My view of the entire sky was restricted, as if I were looking through a large skylight window.

Statues—whose shapes looked as if they should mean something—and pillars and designs made the park resemble a scene from ancient Greece or Rome. It looked like a wonderfully peaceful, happy place. A couple of beings were sitting in the gazebo, and small children played nearby. All of these entities seemed to be part human. I thought I heard children laughing. I tried to focus on the sound, but everything just faded away.

I was instantly back on the craft, and the park was gone. I sort of thumped back into my body. I noticed I felt heavier and realized that I must have been having an out-of-body experience. It had not occurred to me while I was observing the crystal city that I was floating like a spirit.

I was still sitting on the bench with the grays around me. They asked if I liked what I saw. I said I did. I heard the words, "That is where your children will be."

I thought, "What children?"

I was then led into a different room. A door panel slid open. Two small, young humanoids entered the room. A small, female humanoid about 12 or 13 years old and a small, male humanoid about 5 entered the room. As I looked at them closely, I realized that these were also my children! I can only describe this as a telepathic knowing, like "reading a body fingerprint." The children gave off an aura that I recognized as a part of me.

These children looked like pitiful little waifs. They had thin, scraggly hair that looked as if it needed combing. Their eyes were about two to three times the size of human eyes. They looked like those paintings of children with big, sad, oversize eyes that you can order from magazines.

The small boy looked scared. I felt he wanted to hide from me. He did shrink back beside the young girl. The girl smiled slightly, and I felt she knew who I was. I felt a really nice warm feeling inside. I told the boy that I was not going to hurt him. I wanted to touch them and hold them! They were really quite beautiful in a strange sort of way.

I was not allowed to touch them, and they were taken out of the room. I was upset about their leaving. Why had they been brought to me? It was like receiving a beautiful gift, only to have it snatched away as I reached out for it. Why were the grays teasing me in such a cruel way? They seemed oblivious to my emotional state.

A thought/voice said, "Do not worry about them. You will see them again."

At that point I was allowed to leave the craft. I approached my car. I found both of my children asleep inside. I looked back to the craft. The ramp whooshed up into the bottom of the thing, which moved backward out over the valley and disappeared. I got in the car and drove away. I arrived at my destination 90 minutes late.

When Bill brought me out of hypnosis, I was filled with many mixed emotions.

I was amazed at the beautiful city I had seen. Its geometric appearance seemed to produce a peaceful, calm feeling similar to my feeling while seeing the triangle craft when I was 12. It was as if the sheer beauty of the geometric shape of the images created a tranquilizing effect and calmed my soul. I have never had the same feeling from any manmade object.

I felt a deep sadness for these children I hardly knew. I also felt tremendous anxiety for my daughter, who was taken into the craft with me, and for my son, who stayed behind.

The visitors told me not to worry. They should have saved their telepathic breath. Believe me, I worried. I still do. I don't understand what the future holds for any of us. I just know that I love my children. All of them. My seeming inability to protect any of them began to weigh heavily on my mind.

Chapter 11
The Baton Rouge Incident

It is difficult to understand why these experiences are happening to me. When I see that my children may also be involved, a whole new range of emotions come into play. Particularly, the "G" word. Guilt, guilt, guilt! Is it my fault that these experiences are happening to others around me?

In September 1989, Bill hypnotized me again. I remembered riding to a remote area near Baton Rouge, Louisiana, in 1972. I was 17 years old and a runaway. I had attempted to run away from home many times. This time I had made it out of my state and met another young girl, "Lana," (a pseudonym) who traveled with me. We were "hanging out" at a park when we were approached by two boys I will call "Larry" and "Bob."

We talked and flirted for a while, then decided to go for a ride. Larry seemed okay, but Bob annoyed me. He was arrogant and kept trying to grab a feel when he thought he could get away with it. We drove around until it got dark. Someone suggested that we drive out to the woods so we could smoke some marijuana without getting caught.

We took a dirt road out to a remote, wooded area. It was dry, not swampy like so much of southern Louisiana is. We got out of the car and stood around looking into the darkness. Then we all heard a sound in the distance. "Whoop, whoop, whoop..." It sounded electromechanical. It reminded me of the submarine sounds on the TV show *Voyage to the Bottom of the Sea*.

We all began speculating on what it could be. The boys knew the area fairly well. They said there was nothing in the area that would make that kind of sound.

I joked with them. "Maybe it's a UFO!"

Nobody was amused. Bob started to lose his arrogance and appeared frightened. He was not the "he-man" he thought he was.

I noticed some orange lights through the trees in the direction of the sounds. I asked if there was a factory nearby.

Lana said, "No. Maybe we should get out of here."

I said, "Let's go see what it is!" I took off into the trees toward the lights. I heard the guys calling after me to come back.

I walked between some trees and found myself looking up at a row of oval lights. Each light was about a foot wide and two feet long. A chute dropped out from the center of the circle of lights.

I began to feel anxious. I regretted my decision to run into the woods. Four little grays came out of the craft. They wore long vests of a type I had never seen before. A thought-voice in my head said, "Hello, Jeanne."

I felt a mixture of emotions. I was afraid, but part of me was happy to be with them. The Voice said, "You should not have left home." I told them that they were the reason I had left! I thought they would not follow me or bother me any more if I left my hometown.

We prepared to go into the craft. I was no longer afraid, and I hoped that Rainbow would be inside. I wanted to see her. It had been two years since I first saw her.

I stepped into the chute that had dropped down from the craft. I felt a slow spinning sensation as I rose up into the craft. Two grays were waiting for me when I arrived inside. I felt a pressure on my arm as they escorted me into a brightly lit room. The wall was curved and contained bench protrusions.

I noticed a commotion nearby. The grays were bringing Bob into the room. He looked terrified. He screamed at the grays who were with him. He saw me and cried, "Help me!"

Earlier I had felt a smug satisfaction at seeing his bravado crumble. Now his fear made me uncomfortable. I looked at him and said, "You know, it's better if you let them do what they're going to do. It's easier if you don't fight it."

"You're an evil bitch!", he yelled at me.

I told him, "I'm not! It's not my fault!" His words stung me. I thought, "Maybe it is my fault. Maybe he's right." Had I unknowingly posed as bait to lure this boy to the woods?

The grays seemed irritated with Bob, and they moved him away to another room. I heard him screaming and yelling as he disappeared. I felt very bad. I did not like the boy, but I did not want anything bad to happen to him. I wondered what they did to boys. Would he be examined like I had been so many other times?

The grays led me into another room. A large machine stood in the center of this room. Blades spun like the blades of a turbine. There were light panels at the top and bottom. I was told this was a *chromator*, and that it powered the chute that brought me into the craft. They showed it to me as if trying to teach me the purpose of it. I was only mildly interested.

The grays led me into another room and stripped off my clothing. They indicated I was to sit in a partially padded metal chair with arm rests and a head rest. It reminded me of a dentist's chair. I felt very uneasy. I sat down, feeling anxiety rise in me. A clear covering like a plastic dome came over me and the chair.

Suddenly I felt as if I were blasted with electricity! Every part of my body screamed with shock, as if I were being fried from the inside out. My body jerked convulsively, and I thought I was going to explode. The pain seemed to go on forever, but probably only lasted about ten seconds. I know what it must be like to die in the electric chair! It was not a pleasant experience.

Two grays were studying panels and TV screens along one wall near the chair. There was a symbol underneath the row of panels. It looked like Saturn with wavy rings.

I was told that this electric-chair device was a body scan. The "shock" I experienced was some sort of adjustment made at the molecular level. I was told that something had been done to keep me from getting pregnant. (This certainly seemed like a rather extreme method of birth control!) I was told I would become pregnant in a few years. I had to be with the right person at the right time. It could be dangerous for me to become pregnant at the wrong time.

Then I was asked if I would like to see my daughter. I had been thinking about being pregnant, and the grays must have known my thoughts were about Rainbow. I was taken into a small, domed room with a strange gadget in its center. It was like a model of a futuristic Ferris wheel with little spinning stars where the seats would be. I watched this object with some fascination.

A door opened and two female grays brought Rainbow into the room. I felt a sense of happiness coming from these beings. Rainbow seemed scared of me at first. She was smaller than a human toddler of the same age.

I knelt down beside her and said, "It's okay. I'm your Mommy." I took hold of her tiny hand. It felt solid, cool and doll-like. I could not feel any bone structure.

She gave me a half-smile and exuded a "feels good" feeling. I don't know if she was referring to the touch or the experience of being together with me. It was a warm, pleasant moment. I touched her sparse, unruly hair. It felt coarse and wiry. It was very light blonde. I recorded her image into my memory. I sensed it was time to leave. I told her, "I have to go now. Don't forget me!"

I knew the room I was in was her playroom. It seemed like a nice place, just her size. A thought-voice told me, "She's special, just like you are special and all your children are special. You must forget about it for now."

I was taken to the room where I entered the craft. I was lowered to the ground, where a gray stood waiting. He escorted me back to the car. Everyone was standing around the vehicle. There was no movement at first. Then, everyone said, "Let's go!"

I ached and felt stiff. I said, "Let's get out of here." I looked at Bob. He seemed calm and unemotional. We all got into the car and rode back to civilization in silence. No one spoke. We returned to the park to retrieve the other car. I never saw the boys again, and Lana and I never spoke of the incident.

After the hypnosis, I reflected on what I had learned. I enjoyed seeing Rainbow again. She seemed to be doing well at this stage. I hoped they were caring for her properly. She certainly had nice toys! I had been mesmerized by the little Ferris wheel in her room.

Bill, Jean, and I spoke about the electric chair experience. The birth-control explanation seemed implausible to me. Nevertheless, I did not become pregnant until eight years after the incident, despite occasional promiscuity and infrequent use of birth-control measures, and despite deliberate attempts to become pregnant after my marriage later that same year. It just didn't happen. I thought I could never have children. How wrong I was!

Bill and I discussed my guilt feelings. I thought I had gotten the others involved in this strange situation. I did not like the feeling of being "bait". Bob's accusing words still rang in my ears. "Evil Bitch!" Was he right? I didn't feel evil, but knowing that someone thought me evil hurt.

Bill mentioned that Bob had had an instant fear of the lights and sound. Perhaps he had experienced these things before and that was why he was frightened. It made me feel a little better. Maybe we had both been lured. Maybe he lured me there. I may never know for sure.

Chapter 12
Psychoanalyzed

My memories began to return in bits and pieces. Some of the hypnosis sessions provided only small flashes of images. Some of these memories were impossible to place in any definite time frame. Others were easier to date because of the house I lived in or other defining objects nearby. Several incidents occurred during my seventeenth year.

Several months after the Louisiana abduction, a couple of grays came into my room. One gray held my head back while the other pushed a double-pronged gun into each nostril. I felt a searing pain and a sensation of something popping through tissue. It was as if my brain exploded.

I believe some type of device was placed inside my nose or brain. The only residue from that experience was some drainage from my nose to the back of my throat. I don't remember bleeding. I don't remember receiving any other implants, and I would not want to repeat the procedure.

About 15 years later, I was working at a motel as a housekeeper. I had not yet remembered any of my experiences. I was vacuuming the carpet when I felt liquid dripping out of my nose. I put my hand to my nose to see if it was bleeding. I had noticed no signs of a cold or an allergy. On my hand was an orange-brownish stain. I walked over to the vanity. When I bent my head over the sink, liquid poured out of my nose! It had the same color and consistency as iodine or betadine solution. I wiped away the mess and continued with my work. There was no further problem, so I just shrugged it off as "Something Strange." I feel now that this incident may have been connected with my implant in a way I don't understand. It is just one of many strange moments in my life.

The flood of memories began to subside. There were no more feelings of urgency concerning partial memories. The fears I had lived with for so long had lessened considerably. I was feeling more relaxed and positive. I began to assimilate all the information I had learned so far. I continued going to classes at college. Bill Johnson planned for me to undergo a battery of psychological tests to verify that I was sane and coherent. The thought of having my brain picked made me a little nervous, but I agreed. Bill, who worked in the psychiatric department of a local hospital, arranged to have someone who had no knowledge of my experiences test me. The lady was told only that I needed some testing and she was to evaluate any problems that she found.

I thought the tests rather interesting. I was given the Minnesota Multiphasic Personality Inventory—2, the Millon Clinical Multiaxial Inventory, the Thematic Apperception Test, the Weschler Adult Intelligence Scale—Revised, the Gorham Proverb Test, House-Tree-Person Drawing, Kinetic Family Drawing, and the Rotter Incomplete Sentences. I was even given the Rorschach ink-blot test, which I thought was only given to people on TV and in movies!

I registered within the normal ranges on each test. I was found to be somewhat depressed and anxious, but I knew that. There was no hidden psychosis to explain my experiences. I was very relieved that the tests backed me up. I had so often worried that I must be crazy to recall the bizarre memories I had. Well, the memories were crazy, but I was okay!

The IQ sub-test scores entitled me to the verbal, performance, and full-scale intelligence quotients of 117, 119, and 121, respectively. My level of intellectual efficiency was within the superior range. Somewhere below Einstein and above Smart Cookie!

I was glad I was not a psycho, but I was occasionally psychic. At times I had random thoughts or feelings about future events that would come to pass.

The most significant of these occurred in early 1986. I was attending an Army electronics school in Georgia. At the end of one work day, a close friend and I were listening to my car radio on the drive to a restaurant in town. A news broadcast stated that the launch of the Space Shuttle Challenger had been delayed again. I remarked to my friend "It is only a matter of time before one of those things blows up." We launched into a lengthy discussion of what would happen to the space program if such a thing occurred.

The next day the same friend and I walked into the day room of our barracks, and a soldier who had barracks CQ duty approached us.

"Have you heard?" he asked. "The Challenger blew up!"

Shocked and spooked, my friend and I hurried to where a television was replaying the day's events. I could not believe it. Why had I said what I said about a shuttle blowing up? Where had that thought come from? I have not ignored any such passing thoughts since that day. Whenever I feel apprehension about something, I say so!

My psychic abilities are random and unpredictable. I have come to believe that there is no such thing as coincidence. Everything happens for a reason, and I take coincidences very seriously. I wish I had greater control of the times I know when something is going to happen. I never know until after the fact. It is not very helpful—just eerie.

I have had other strange experiences that may or may not be related to abductions. It is difficult to discern whether the activity is alien-related or caused by some obnoxious poltergeist or spirit entity. Who can tell?

One time I was cooking fried chicken and turning the pieces with a heavy antique metal fork. I set the fork down on the counter and walked into the other room to watch television. A few minutes later, I returned to the kitchen to turn the chicken again. I picked up the fork and noticed one of the middle tines was bent straight up! I tried to bend it back. I could not do it. No one was in the house but me.

Another time, an "unbreakable" dinner plate flew out of my cupboard and shattered into thousands of tiny glass slivers. It landed on carpet and seemed to explode rather than break. I constantly drop things in the corner of the kitchen where this happened. I am unable to keep a grip on any object in that area of the house!

One day, at the factory where I was working, a long fluorescent light exploded above me. Only five other people were in the plant at the time. Many times I have walked into rooms and have seen the lights begin to glow more brightly. This often happens when I am deep in thought about something. It is as if the energy of my thoughts influences the electrical field in the room.

One day my boss was working on a television in a room I was cleaning. We both were sure the lamp was on above the dresser on which the TV sat. As we were leaving the room, my boss realized he had forgotten to do something. We re-entered the room and tried to turn on the lamp. When nothing happened, I checked to see if the light bulb had burned out. There was no bulb there—just an empty socket!

Two years ago, I ran out of propane gas at my home. I turned off all pilot lights and the main valve on the tank outside. The gas man came, filled the tank, and asked me if I needed help relighting the pilots. I told him I knew how to do it and I would do it later because I was leaving to run some errands. I left the house.

When I returned four hours later, I decided to take a nap. When I awoke several hours later, it was beginning to get dark and cold outside. I walked outside and turned on the main valve of the propane tank. I walked back into the house to light the pilot lights on my gas range. They were all already lit! No one had been in the house. I know the pilots had been out completely that morning. I still have a problem figuring this one out!

I stopped wearing quartz battery watches because my body seemed to affect them strangely. The hands would start spinning around very fast, indicating the passage of an hour about every fifteen minutes! I noticed the same thing happened to my date's watch one night. We were amazed at what was happening.

I attribute many experiences to my psychic/spiritual awakening.

So much of my self has opened up, including my creativity. I began drawing and painting again—strange images that looked like cell structures, physics theories, or star charts. Sometimes I wrote accompanying explanations. I felt the same feeling while drawing these images as I did while receiving the telepathic messages.

I fell in love with words and language. I started writing poetry. I had written a few poems before, but only on rare occasions. Sometimes, instead of telepathic communications, I felt compelled to write poetry or lyrics. The words flowed through me, and I had to put them on paper.

One of the first poems I wrote during this time is about the entities who have become a part of my life. I don't know why I wrote it with a Celtic tone. I am very fond of this particular poem, and I want to share it with you:

Night Visitors

Into the silent maze of sleep
Come thund'ring kings of nightly quest,
Conquering the slumbering thought,
Helpless in its weary nest.
Flitting forms of phantom visions
Dance the dance of faery wind,
Starlight fancy, noble princes
Briefly spent, and gone again.
Nocturnal visits unannounced,
Plundering the fruitful host,
Reaping children of the future
Leaving only memory's ghost.
Darkness passes at day's dawning;
World awakens with the sun;
Mystery spirits have departed
Satisfied their work is done.

Chapter 13
Debbie and I

In October 1989, Bill Johnson informed me that he had been invited to speak at a conference in Aspen, Colorado. He told me several well-known abductees were to participate in a panel discussion. Included on this panel were Betty Hill, Travis Walton, Charles Hickson, and Debbie Jordan ("Kathie Davis" of Budd Hopkins' book, *Intruders*).

I was deeply envious of Bill. I would have loved to talk to these people who remembered experiences similar to my own—particularly to Debbie. Many of my experiences seemed to parallel hers. I wished Bill well and told him to tell Debbie hello for me if he got an opportunity.

I eagerly awaited word from Bill. He called me soon after his return and excitedly related all he had learned from the conference. He had talked with Debbie at great length about her experiences. Strangely enough, she also had been receiving and writing down telepathic information on many subjects. Some of the information she received was nearly a match of my own!

I was amazed, excited, and blown away by this news. I didn't feel nearly as strange after learning someone else was having the same experiences. I thought, "I may be strange, but at least I have company!" Bill said Debbie felt the same way. He gave me Debbie's address and said she wanted me to write her.

I was so excited! There were so many things I had wanted to tell her since reading *Intruders* so long ago. I wanted her to know of the feelings her story evoked in me, but I had never expected to have an opportunity to tell her.

I immediately set out to write a letter. I was not sure how to begin. She seemed like such a regular person in the book. I was moderately intimidated, but the words poured out of me. I hoped they would sound coherent. I wrote many pages of feelings that I had kept to myself for so long, and it felt good! I felt that if anyone would understand, Debbie would.

Several days later I received a letter from her! When I saw it, I had to laugh. All over the outside of the envelope were Greenpeace stickers! The letter I had mailed to her was covered with them, also! Debbie obviously felt the same awareness and desire to protect the environment.

I tore into the letter and began reading. She had written nearly the same feelings as I expressed to her! She was down-to-earth, intelligent, and level-headed. I was happy to find she was normal and not of the lunatic fringe. Her salty language and tell-it-as-I-see-it attitude was wonderfully refreshing.

We began writing to each other regularly. We discovered that many symbols we had drawn matched each other. Several of the telepathic communications were nearly identical. It was great to be able to share experiences and the feelings behind them. We began to evaluate what was happening in hope of making sense of it all.

I was continuing to receive telepathic communications almost daily. The information I was receiving began to get technical and more complex. I did not understand the words or the meanings that were being given to me. I continued to write them down. I sent them to Bill Johnson, hoping he could make some sense of them.

One day, while I was on a break from school, I felt an urge to draw a group of dots and circles on a piece of paper. It looked like a constellation of stars after I had finished it. I decided to send it to Bill with everything else.

The first technical message I received was a surprise to me. I looked at what I had written and laughed. I wondered what it could mean. Was it just some techno-babble that had no purpose behind it? This is what it said:

> *Cyclotronic generation of adjusted flux in cohesion with elemental fusion of inherent DNA. In addition, photon diffusion pertaining to the coefficient of the altered properties is essential for quantum movement in relation to time and space continuum.*

This was strange but fun! It was so bizarre and out of my range of thinking. What if someone could figure it out? What if it actually meant something? That would certainly prove to me that my experience was real. I knew I had no great understanding of science. I was fascinated by it but only on a very simple level.

Bill decided to send a sampling of these communications to a physicist for analysis. The physicist, Dave, was not able to decipher the messages, but he did not discount them. He did write to Bill and mentioned that the "star chart" I had drawn was almost identical to the systems around the Andromeda Galaxy. Only a couple of "stars" were missing or misplaced.

Dave made a list of questions for me to ask or contemplate in hopes of further clarification. I doubted that I would get any answers to these questions, but I decided to try just for the sport of it. I held the questions in my mind and waited for any response. I began to get answers to most of these questions. They came in a random order over a period of about two weeks:

Q: What is "cyclotronic generation of adjusted flux?"

A: *Alteration of DNA complex by stimulation of nuclei using controlled generation of electromagnetic waves.*

Q: What is "photon diffusion?"

A: *A grafting of light energy into the substance and molecular alignment of a bioplasm.*

Q: What is "the coefficient of the altered properties?"

A: *The amount of change in molecular adjustment after being energized with electromagnetic pulse in which flux radius alters atomic number of cell reproduction and regeneration.*

Q: What is the M# (man's scientific registration) of the galaxy you come from?

A: *13, 31, 14.*

(I did not know what he was talking about, but I mentioned that I felt 13 was where the grays were from and 31 & 14 were where the colonies were located.)

Q: What is "angel hair"?

A: *Angel hair is the sloughing off of a protective emulsion emitted by our craft's external systems device. It is constantly generated to protect against contaminants. When it has reached maximum absorption levels, it is discarded. It is protection from the many pollutants in your atmosphere. It also serves as an outer lubricant to relieve external stress caused by atmospheric friction.*

Bill gave Debbie some of the same questions and compared her answers to mine. Debbie and I were not allowed to compare answers until each of us completed the series of questions. Some of the answers were eerily similar.

Q: What is the purpose of implants?

A: (Jeanne) *The sensory implants have many uses. They are tracking devices. They record sensory input from the subjects. They register pollution levels in the subject. They measure stress levels. We are able to study the migrational habits of your people. It enables us to communicate with our test subjects, even from great distances.*

A: (Debbie) *Tracking, monitoring of individual and sensory receptors, and occasionally altering the energy level of the individual to facilitate necessary communications and molecular changes for the greater good through adjustment of energy levels.*

Q: How do you use light?

A: (Jeanne) *We travel by means of light fusion. We are able to travel great distances using this power. You were brought on board our craft by means of spectral transport. Your essence was blended with the light beam. It is one method of matter transference. The light particles penetrate your atomic structure, which is recorded into the transposer memory. Matter is then reconstructed at the desired site of appearance. Light penetration of matter causes matter to become light which can be controlled and directed to the chosen area of reintegration.*

A: (Debbie) *Light, in its many forms, can be used in many different ways: nutrition, healing tissue, travel, disassemble molecules/pass through light/reassemble, light as a means of self-propulsion.*

Q: How do you eat and/or drink?

A: (Jeanne) *Our method of consumption is very different from your own. We absorb what we need from our environment (and yours). It is similar to photosynthesis. We need light, mineral substances not existing on your planet, proteins, and moisture.*

A: (Debbie) *Absorption through the outer covering of the body—skin—through the soft tissue inside the mouth. Energy ray, nutritional fluids. Waste excreted through the skin. We do not drink as you understand drink —do not "swallow." Fluid is absorbed through tissue in "mouth".*

Q: Do you have music, comedy, theater?

A: (Jeanne) *Our music is the music of light and visual images. Geometric combinations and light patterns are pleasing and soothing to the soul. Theater is used for educational purposes, such as giving of examples for various situations. It is not for entertainment. We do not have comedy in a theatrical sense. We have humor and amusement. You are an amusing species.*

A: (Debbie) *Music is vital, theater and comedy understood. You are our theater—our comedy.*

It is difficult to convey the feeling when experiences, symbols, or communications match up with those of another person who lives hundreds of miles away. When someone's drawings or words match exactly to your own, it slams this reality home. You ask yourself "If this is not real, why are we seeing and experiencing the same things?"

When this happens over and over again, it is difficult to deny that something is happening—something that needs to be investigated, not ridiculed. I know something strange is happening to me. It doesn't matter if no one else believes me. I believe in myself, and that's what counts.

Chapter 14
Feeding Time

Several times, as a youngster, I noticed a strong odor on my hands and a brown substance under my fingernails. I recalled that this substance smelled similar to beans and onions. I had not eaten anything that would have left this residue on my hands.

For some reason, memories of those childhood incidents came back to me while I was listening to a boring lecture at college. I knew this was significant. Later that day I wrote a letter to Bill Johnson and told him about the memories. Bill told me that smell is the only one of the five senses we cannot voluntarily control. We can choose not to use all of the others. We can close our eyes. We can avoid touch, taste, and sound. Smell happens. It is there before we realize it. Smell is a good memory trigger.

I felt the need for another hypnosis session. I wanted to find out what the substance on my hands could be. We scheduled a time to meet. Under hypnosis, I began to remember a night when I was about ten years old.

I had awakened to the sound of someone calling my name. I got out of bed and walked into the night. I stood in my front yard feeling a bit scared. This feeling deepened as I watched a ring of lights appear in the sky above me.

I heard a low humming noise as the circle of lights moved closer. As I stood there, a bluish-purple beam came out of the center of the lights and engulfed me. When the light hit me, I felt numb and tingly. Then I was inside a room, where several of the familiar, gray beings waited for me.

"Don't be afraid." a thought-voice said.

I was told to lie on a nearby table. I was terrified when one of the grays pulled down my pajama bottoms to examine me. The creature pressed on my abdomen and looked at me closely. Another gray moved its hand over my chest. I shivered with the chill of it. A thought appeared in my mind that they were checking my development.

One of the grays had an insignia on its form-fitted clothing. It was a circle with a yellow wave or wing with a black stripe through the wing.

I was allowed to sit up after the examination. As I readjusted my pajamas, another gray entered the room. This one wore a purple, high-collared cape that seemed to be attached with a jeweled, starburst clasp in the front.

I recognized this creature when he strode into the room. It was the gray I had called "Grandpa" when I was four years old. His personality and presence filled the room the moment he entered. He looked physically like all the others, but he had a powerful presence. I felt no personality at all from the other workers. I was not afraid of Grandpa Gray.

I heard a thought-voice say, "It is good to see you." He then asked me how I was and if I would like to go into another room. I said yes.

The next room was dark, except for a light coming from several large windows. I walked over to the nearest one. What I saw made me gasp with surprise! It was a beautiful blue planet with white swirls of clouds. It was the earth! For a moment I felt as if I were going to fall. I almost threw up from the sudden vertigo I felt as I looked out the window.

The being looked at me, and his voice was in my head. "This is how your earth looks."

I said, "How high up are we?" The thought of a thousand miles appeared in my head. I asked this being if he had a name. I heard a sound like "Queet zow." Queetzal?

Queetz then told me that I was special, and I should remember that. He said I was a part of something very special, and that was why they came to see me. He asked me if I would like to do a special job. It was something they needed me to do.

We stepped into a small room, and the door shut behind us. Queetzal moved his hand over a light panel. I felt movement. We seemed to be in a type of elevator. The sensation of movement felt horizontal, not vertical. We stopped and entered a brightly lit room.

In front of me was a row of little boxes or beds coming out of the wall. As I moved closer, I noticed babies in the beds—tiny little creatures that seemed to be mixtures of human and gray. I counted eight of these little infants.

As I was looking at them, I noticed a bed behind the others. As I focused on it, I realized I was looking at a grossly deformed "thing"—and it was staring back at me! I panicked. I wanted to come out of hypnosis immediately! What I saw horrified me.

I don't know what it was, but it was alive. It looked like some terrible mistake of creation. Just as I felt the fear reach an uncontrollable level, a screen came up over my eyes. When I looked again, it was just another baby like the others. Once the horror was gone, I was able to relax and continue with the hypnosis.

I asked Queetz if these babies were his. He said, "They belong to all of us. Do you want to feed them?" I was indifferent, but I said okay. I did not want to hurt his feelings!

Two grays in another part of the room were busily preparing something. It was a bowl of a foul-smelling brown substance. The smell was very offensive. It smelled like onions, garlic, beans, and some other odors I could not identify. The substance was the color and thickness of apple butter.

I was led to an opening in one of the walls. Queetz indicated I was to put my hands in this opening. I hesitated for a moment, "Is this going to hurt?" I was told that this window produced a disinfectant to clean my hands. I placed my hands inside and felt a mist, like cool steam, on my hands.

I stepped back and we moved over to the first little bed. The baby was very small and thin. Its head seemed too big for its body. It looked like a baby bird. I could almost see its internal organs through its thin skin. The little creature looked at me. A gray held the bowl, and I received a thought that I was to stick my hands in this substance and rub it on the baby. I was to rub it on the chest, arms, stomach and back, like lotion!

I wrinkled my nose and scooped out a handful of goo and rubbed it into the baby's skin. I was to keep rubbing until it disappeared. I smiled and said, "He likes it!" I could feel the pleasure of the baby as I rubbed the food into his skin.

I was told, "It satisfies two hungers. It feeds him nutrients and eases the hunger for touching."

I asked them, "Why don't you just sit him in the bowl?" I received a thought that the baby would drown/suffocate, and it would not work that way.

I moved to another little bed. This baby looked different. It seemed a little more human, and it was female. She had some hair on her head, and her eyes were human, but slightly larger than normal. This child was larger than the first.

I was told to feed this one differently. I rubbed some of the brown stuff on this child, but I was also given a bag to feed it by mouth. The bag looked like the funnel tubes that are used for decorating cakes. There was a clear liquid in the tube. I placed the tip in the baby's mouth, and she sucked at it. She made a squeaky sound as she drank from the bag.

The first baby I fed and one other looked like little grays. The rest looked mostly human. I was told the two were very special babies. They get "special, special care." Queetzal told me that they needed our help to make more babies. There are not enough of them to survive. They cannot reproduce quickly enough.

When I was finished rubbing down the last baby, one of the grays turned a bright light on over them. I asked Queetz, "Do you have to bake them now?"

His thoughts told me, "They need the light. It helps them digest." As I observed, I had the feeling that I was participating in this because it would be my job someday. I did not understand this thought, but I did not question it.

Soon it was time for me to leave. Queetzal took me out of the room, and we made our way back to the window room. We stopped there for a moment. He looked into my eyes. His thoughts told me to be strong—that he would watch out for me. He told me not to feel bad and not to forget I am special.

We entered a little room, and I stood on a platform in the middle. As Queetz raised his hand in a wave, I began to feel very tired. The next thing I recalled was being back in my yard. I walked inside the house and went back to bed.

Bill brought me out of the hypnosis, and we discussed what had occurred. It seemed so strange. Their manner of eating was odd, but it seemed to make sense. I felt good about this experience. They did not seem like such bad creatures. Queetzal seemed so protective of me. I had often felt protected and special as a child; maybe this was the reason.

That special feeling disappeared once I became a teenager. I felt used up. I remain confused about the experiences. Sometimes I feel I am part of some Grand Purpose. At other times I get angry with the loss of control. I would feel so much better if I were given the choice to participate. If I did make this choice, I wish I could remember. I would like to lose the resentment. I felt love from this Queetzal being. I try not to forget that.

Chapter 15
Butterfly Dance

In my continuing quest for knowledge, I felt I was being led to books and information on reincarnation and the continuation of the soul. I had considered the idea of past lives but never related the stories to any personal involvement. I felt drawn to certain periods of history, but I had no specific memories of any earlier lives. The idea remained a possibility.

One book I read referred to soul mates—couples who felt they were born to be together during many lifetimes. I thought this a wonderfully romantic notion—two loving souls choosing to live life after life together.

This was a concept that was beyond my comprehension. So many of my relationships ended after a few weeks or months; eternity was out of the question! Nevertheless, I remained hopeful. I had always felt there was a very special soul waiting for me somewhere—someone I had been aware of since my childhood. I had dreams of a man who knew me very well and loved me anyway. All my life I had subconsciously talked with someone—a secret friend who always listened and who was always supportive. During times when I felt sad or lonely, I would talk to this invisible companion, and he would understand me completely. For years, I assumed that this person was imaginary. I had not yet met anyone who felt like this invisible friend.

As time passed, books I read and songs I listened to reminded me of my mystery person. My mind would return to the man who haunted my dreams. I felt a deep longing for him. I often was attracted to men who resembled my dream buddy, only to realize they were not The One. Where was he? Did he exist?

In the fall of 1989, I began to have flashes of memory of an experience on a craft with another human. There was a feeling of participating in an arranged encounter with a special person. I did not have a vivid image of this man at first—only bits of memory that were beginning to increase.

Could this memory be a connection to my secret friend? I tried to recall the image of the man on the craft and compared the memories to the man who appeared in my dreams. I knew his spirit and personality, but I could not get a clear picture of his face. I became increasingly convinced that the person on the craft and the person in my dreams were the same man.

I buried the feelings inside myself and tried to forget them, but my emotions kept surfacing in my dreams. It inspired me to keep looking and wondering. Was he real? Was he thinking about me?

Meanwhile, each of my relationships lasted only a few days or months or years. Each one would begin with great promise, then, gradually, one of us would realize we were wasting our time. Inwardly, I knew how great love could be. Time and again I lost interest when the relationship failed to meet my expectations. More often than not, I did not meet my partner's expectations either. Once I realized the person was not The One, I cooled considerably and quit trying.

I was very frustrated because I did not know who I was missing. I had a reasonably clear idea of what had happened on the craft, but I could not remember the man's physical appearance, and some parts of my memories were confused with other events I had recalled under hypnotic regression. Eventually I was able to piece dreams and conscious memories together into a more complete picture:

I was led into a rather dimly lit room. A short distance away, two grays were tending instruments on a panel board. They seemed to be in a slightly elevated side room connected to the room I was in. The only object that I noticed in my section of the room was a type of table or bench.

I stood there, naked, observing the situation, beginning to get frightened of what might come next. Usually I was taken for an exam, then taught or shown something.

This was not the typical examination area. Exam rooms usually resembled brightly lit doctors' offices. This room was different. It was lit with a diffused, blue light coming from several rectangular paneled areas near the ceiling. The upper-level room where the grays worked was brightly lit, but its light did not seem to penetrate into this room.

I stood with my back to the thigh-high table and watched the grays. They moved about busily without paying me any attention. Did they know I was there? I sensed some activity off to my right and turned to look.

A door had opened. A gray was escorting a naked human male into the room. I remember thinking, "Thank God he's human!" (I assumed he was human.) He was tall and very slim. He seemed to tower above the gray who accompanied him. He had light brown hair that just barely touched his shoulders.

As I was evaluating this fellow, I realized he was looking at me. That first moment of eye contact sent a shock wave through me! I was still frightened, but I felt excitement also. The gray brought the man to where I was standing. I knew telepathically that the man and I were supposed to join together on the platform/table behind me. Nothing was said, but that was the image that appeared in my mind when the gray looked at me. I assumed this meant sex.

The gray left us standing there and walked over to the side room where the others were working. I watched it go and then turned back to the man. Could I run and get away? I felt like a deer caught in headlights. I was scared but unable to move.

The man seemed to sense my fear. He smiled slightly and said, "I won't hurt you."

As I looked into his eyes, I found that I believed him. He was very nice looking, and I no longer wanted to run. I wanted to say something, but I could not form the words. I smiled back at him. We looked at each other for a few awkward minutes.

A very gentle feeling seemed to radiate from him. I felt a strong attraction toward him, and I could see that the feeling was mutual. He seemed to be struggling inwardly with his response to me. I felt something on a telepathic level, but I did not realize what it was at first.

I wanted to tell him it was okay. I was no longer afraid, and I wanted him to touch me. The feeling may have been induced, but it felt very natural. I still could not speak, so I reached up and touched his cheek lightly. We maintained steady eye contact, and very strong feelings were passed between us.

The man touched my shoulder and moved his hand down to the side of my breast. I could not stop smiling. He leaned over and kissed me very gently. I felt as if I had been hit by a lightning bolt! We responded to each other with a growing intensity. At this point, the recollection gets hazy. Somehow we both were lying on the table in the center of the room. For a moment I was distracted from my feelings and noticed that the strange gray visitors were watching us intently. My fear returned as I realized what was happening. The man looked in the same direction and saw the grays staring at us with those deep, black eyes. The sight of them seemed to unsettle him.

He moved his hand to my face and turned it away from the grays and towards him. "Don't look at them," he said. "Look into my eyes and forget about them. It's just the two of us here alone." He seemed to be trying to convince himself of this idea also. He spoke with an accent, but I could not distinguish what kind it was.

When we looked into each other's eyes again, my fear disappeared. I'm not sure what happened next. Somehow we were joined together. I don't know if this joining was an actual physical act as well as a spiritual experience, but that first moment of connection was exquisite! Something changed within us and around us, and all I was aware of was this beautiful person who was suddenly a part of me.

We seemed to blend into each other. I knew everything he was feeling. We knew each other completely. I realized what "knowing" someone in the Biblical sense was all about. I used to laugh at that term, but now I understand what it actually means. It is a very accurate description of this physical/spiritual experience.

All the emotions this man had ever felt flowed through me. All the feelings of loneliness, pleasure, fear, pain, and happiness were a part of me. I did not know the details of his life, but I knew the emotions that had brought him to this moment.

He felt like me! We had the same emotional design. We had the same desires, fears, and hopes. I was overwhelmed by the feelings of finding the man who was my perfect match. It was as if we were two sides of a broken coin that had been rejoined in seamless perfection. We were one soul; he was the male half and I was the female. We were Yin and Yang—complete. The ecstatic feeling went far beyond the physical.

I don't know how long this experience lasted. When we returned to our separate selves, we were clinging to each other trying to recapture our breath. I heard myself say, "I love you." Those were the first words I spoke to him.

"I love you, too," he told me, smiling.

I felt really happy for once in my life. The feeling didn't last long. I noticed a stirring and movement in the room. The grays! I forgot they were there! They were coming over to us. I felt a sudden surge of indescribable panic.

"Don't leave me! I need you!" I whispered to him. The grays were standing near us now.

"We can find each other! I won't forget you, and I won't stop looking 'til I find you!" His voice had a tone of urgency that I understood completely. The grays took him by the arm and led him toward the door.

"I'll remember!" I called after him, as the door shut between us. Several of the grays appeared to be taking readings from hand-held instruments. One pressed a metal object against my abdomen and moved it across me. I barely noticed. All I could think of was that I was alone again. I had found the man I had been looking for for so long—and had lost him again! I cursed myself for forgetting to ask his name. Now he was gone.

Several years ago, I recalled a memory that I feel is connected to the man I met on the craft. The event took place near the time of my first experience with the visitors or perhaps during that first abduction. I was very young—about four years old.

I was in a room on a craft, watching a procedure being performed on a young boy. The boy appeared to be about 12 years old. Several grays were in the room. One was holding the boy while another was sticking some metal instrument into the child's left ear. The boy was crying during the procedure, and I felt very sad for him.

I was standing nearby, holding my old, stretched-out sock monkey that my grandmother made for me. I assume I was allowed to bring this toy with me when I was taken aboard the craft. I called the monkey "Booger Eyes." It was my security object and my favorite toy. I carried it everywhere with me, and it was stretched thin and worn.

I silently and solemnly watched the gray work on the boy. After the procedure was finished, the two of us were left alone together in the room. The boy was still crying. I walked up to him and, without a word, handed him my precious toy. I felt sad for the boy and knew he was frightened. The monkey was my security, and it always made me feel safer to hold it. I thought my monkey would make him feel better. The boy took the toy and stopped crying. He seemed to understand the meaning behind the gift. I don't recall whether either of us spoke during this exchange. It seemed as if we understood each other without having to speak.

I don't know if the boy kept my toy, but I never saw my monkey again. What happened to Booger Eyes has been a family mystery. No one knew what happened to this favorite toy of mine. It just disappeared. My grandmother made me a new stuffed monkey to take its place. This new toy looked like Booger Eyes, but it was well stuffed and stiff and I wanted nothing to do with it. It was not Booger Eyes, and I didn't want a replacement. I find myself wondering if I'll ever see that toy again. Perhaps it is in an Earth toy museum on some other planet. I will never know.

I feel that this boy was the same person who shared the special bonding experience with me later in life. It seems as if we were brought together very early in our lives, then brought together again as adults. I feel we had an empathic connection with each other during this early encounter also. I know I felt the boy's sadness as if it were my own. I have no other recollections of meeting this familiar stranger who appeared in my life, but it feels as if I have always known him. I know I would recognize him were I to see him again. Mostly I would know the feel of him. His spirit was much clearer to me than his face.

I have filed these memories away with all the other strange happenings of my life. I really thought it would be only a short time before we found each other again. I thought the telepathic connection would be like some type of inner radar that would bring us back together. I really thought it would be that easy.

I think about him often. When I see a familiar face in a crowd, I wonder. The possibility of crossing paths with him now seems remote, but I believe in miracles, and if miracles can happen to some people, maybe one will happen for me.

Even if I were to find him, what would I say? I know how hazy these memories are. He may not even remember. I could not envision myself approaching someone with, "Hi, Babe! Didn't we meet on a UFO?" Yeah, right. I don't think so. So many impossible barriers between us. How would we ever know for sure?

As time passes, this experience remains my favorite memory. I will never forget the man. I don't understand these feelings I have about him. What does it all mean? I see him in my dreams on a continuing basis. I feel he is as aware of me as I am of him. Maybe he is struggling with his own hazy memories.

One warm fall day, I was thinking of him and wondering if we would see each other again. I saw two beautiful, yellow butterflies flutter lazily across the lawn. One came from the east, and one from the west. They met and circled each other in a butterfly dance. After a brief moment, they separated and flew off in opposite directions. I watched them depart. My missing friend and I were like those butterflies. That one moment in time may be all we ever have. Just a little bit of butterfly love to cherish and remember. I will remember.

I must mention that I have changed a couple of the details of this incident on the craft. That is for my protection. The only person who would know the difference is the man who shared the experience with me.

This memory is an endless source of inspiration. I can tap into the emotion of it whenever I need a spark of love and hope. I have written more than twenty poems and songs about the experience. I will share one with you. It accurately describes how I feel today. This is for my elusive love—the one who got away. Wherever you are, whoever you are, I will not forget you.

Looking For Him

She doesn't know the whole story.
She doesn't know his name.
All she knows are her feelings.
Does he feel the same?
Clinging to dreams
Of a love far away,
One day he'll find her,
But it won't be today.
She's missing someone.
She doesn't know who.
She'll never stop looking,
'Cause that's all she can do.
She's growing older,
But she doesn't forget.
Love can move mountains,
So she'll never quit
Looking for him.
Where is he?
Who is he?
Who is the man
Who has stolen her heart?
One day they'll meet
Face to face
On the street.
That's when the lovin' will start.

Maybe she's crazy and wasting her life.
Maybe he's married and in love with his wife.
Maybe it's all just a warm fantasy,
Until she knows, she will never be free.

Chapter 16
New Friends

As months passed, I uncovered all the urgent memories that needed to surface. The time between hypnosis sessions grew longer. I explored most of the odd memories that had plagued me over the years. The questionable areas that remained were not bothering me, so I left them alone.

Debbie Jordan and I continued to write each other often. We developed a comfortable friendship through our letters. We made plans to meet each other someday. We considered picking a city that was a halfway point between our two locations. St. Louis was a logical choice, as each of us would have to drive only about four hours.

One day Bill Johnson contacted me. He told me that a St. Louis UFO study group had offered Debbie and me a chance to meet each other. This group would put us up in a hotel if we would jointly meet with their group and talk about our experiences.

I jumped at the opportunity! I thought it was a great idea. I told Bill yes and deeply hoped Debbie felt the same way. Soon after, I heard that everything was arranged and agreed upon. Debbie was excited about the meeting also. We agreed on a date that was convenient for all of us.

On April 18, 1990, I arrived at the motel with Bill Johnson and another of his assistants, Carla. We got settled into our rooms while Bill made some phone calls. I was happy to learn that Debbie and I were to share a room. That would give us more time to talk. I was a little nervous about the UFO meeting that was scheduled for later in the evening.

Debbie arrived a short time later. It was a great feeling to meet her face to face. I knew we were kindred spirits when I looked into her eyes. One talent I gained from the ET experience is the ability to read people's personalities. I can tell when someone wears a mask. I can sense someone who is pretending to be what they are not. Debbie and I "read" each other very quickly. I think we each recognized what the other was doing. It was the beginning of a strong psychic bond between us, and it is the basis for a very honest relationship.

We began discussing the similarities in our lives and sharing weird stories. The feelings poured out. It was so good to have someone to talk to who understood what I was feeling. Three years earlier I had read *Intruders* and wished I could talk to this woman. I got my wish. We talked for a while before we began to unpack and get settled into the room.

Debbie dug into her bag and pulled out a crystal pyramid. She had brought it for me. I was so amazed! I had remembered an abduction experience during which the grays had attempted to teach me psychokinesis. The creatures had a crystal pyramid, and they wanted me to move it with the power of my mind. I could only move it a short distance, but I was fascinated with the pyramid.

Since that time, I had drawn pyramids of various types on any paper I had handy. I wanted to find a crystal pyramid like the one I had recalled. I began scanning the shops for anything similar. It was really strange when Debbie popped this beautiful little pyramid out of her bag! It was just one of many coincidences that would happen in our lives.

(I am sorry to report that the pyramid disappeared from my house several years ago. I was very upset when I noticed it was gone. I turned the house upside down looking for it. Several other small items were missing as well. I hope it burned the fingers of the one who took it!)

We went to a restaurant for a bite to eat and then prepared to attend the meeting. I am always anxious before meeting new people. The feelings and emotions that people radiate can be overwhelming at times.

I was introduced to several St. Louis people who have since become very good friends. Two of the persons I met in St. Louis were Jo Palermo and Forest Crawford.

Jo has been a good friend to me and a person I can trust. I don't see him often, but he has a genuine friendliness that I deeply appreciate.

I liked Forest instantly, and that feeling deepened when I realized we had several things in common. We both were drawn to Native American spirituality, and we both liked listening to the Moody Blues!

Forest and Bill Johnson had been formulating questions to "ask the aliens." This was an effort to gather information that many abductees, including Debbie and me, were receiving telepathically. The answers to these questions contained many similarities.

After everyone introduced themselves at the meeting, Debbie and I took turns talking about our experiences. We included some of the "communications" we had received. We were surprised at the similarity between our answers. The discussion turned into a question-and-answer session for Debbie and me.

One of the questions concerned the babies that we had seen on alien craft. Our babies. I felt panic rise in me. I was not prepared for the emotions I was feeling. I didn't know these people very well, and it was a very personal and painful memory. It took Debbie a fraction of a second to see what I was feeling, and I did not have to say a word.

Debbie requested a bathroom break for us. It was just what I needed to keep myself from hyperventilating. We discussed the feelings we both had about our children and the difficulties we had talking about them. I began to feel better and stronger.

That was the first time I noticed the strength of our combined energy. It was a strength that I feel growing each time I get together with other experiencers. It is the feeling of instinctually knowing a shared truth. We may not have any answers, but we know what we have seen. This shared knowledge gives us strength when we are faced with a smirking, ridiculing public. They can laugh until their sides split, but we know what is out there. We may not know what it means, but it certainly is not a joking matter.

The St. Louis group was kind and friendly, and I realized they were not going to ridicule us. They were curious, and they wanted to learn more. We spent the rest of the evening sharing all aspects of our experiences with them. It felt so very good to be able to speak openly about my experiences. When we returned to our hotel room after the meeting, we stayed up late talking about anything and everything.

The weekend with Debbie ended much too quickly. She invited me to come visit her in Indiana, and then we parted company sadly. I felt a little empty spot inside me when I left. I knew Deb and I would see each other again, but I already missed the connection she and I had established together. It was even more obvious when we separated.

In the years since our meeting, Deb and I have developed a very comfortable friendship. We are different people who have grown up in different environments, but we are very much alike in understanding. We are like sisters; we may not agree on everything, but a bond exists between us that cannot be broken.

I love every opportunity I get to spend time with Debbie. When we are together, we grow a little stronger. We learn a little more. We share a lot of laughter, a few tears, and a continually growing hope for a better future.

I was slowly beginning to meet other people who had recalled experiences that were similar to mine. I felt very close and connected to some of these people, but some I could not relate to at all. I heard a wide array of stories from many different people. Some of these experiences rang true, while others seemed too far out to believe. I have gradually learned to listen objectively to people and trust my instincts about what is true and what is not. I try to understand what the experiences are telling me about the person involved, without being too critical. None of us knows all of the truth, but we have a great opportunity to learn from each other.

Several months after meeting Debbie, I was invited to participate in the filming of a documentary about UFOs and abductions. I was nervous about this possibility, so I was not sure I was going to say anything about my experiences in front of a camera.

The documentary was being produced by Linda Moulton Howe. I was told that she was well known for her research into the cattle-mutilation phenomenon. I had seen photos of animal mutilations in the media, and I got an eerie, uneasy feeling looking at the strange, bloodless damage done to the animals. The connection between UFOs and these mutilations worried me a little.

The filming was taking place at the rural home of a couple who had had many unusual UFO experiences. Several people were already at this location when I arrived. Bill Johnson was there with some of his assistants. Shortly after I arrived, Bill introduced me to Linda Howe.

At this first meeting, I sensed Linda had a very strong personality and a very inquisitive mind. I found myself opening up to her and telling her many aspects of my experiences that I usually kept to myself. She explained to me some her ideas for the documentary she was making.

The filming went well. I was fascinated with all the behind-the-scenes technology that was required to create a finished product. I was filmed with several other abductees as we sat at the kitchen table. We began to discuss and compare our experiences for the first time. It was strange talking about the experiences in front of the camera crew. I am sure they thought we were pretty strange, but they were polite and did their job without making us feel too uncomfortable. All in all, it was a very interesting evening.

I have kept in contact with Linda over the years, and I share information with her from time to time. I value her opinions and insights, and I am grateful that she has included me in several of her projects. It has been quite an educational experience, and it has helped me to conquer some deep fears of speaking in public.

In October 1990, I attended my first UFO conference in St. Louis, Missouri. I was very excited about going because several well known speakers were going to be there. Linda Moulton Howe was speaking, as was Budd Hopkins. I was finally going to meet Mr. Hopkins three years after I wrote him the series of anxious letters. When I was introduced to Budd, I found him to be a very kind, gentle man with a pleasant sense of humor. I liked him immediately. I was so grateful that he had read my letters and connected me to Bill Johnson. During that weekend, people constantly gathered around him to talk. I didn't want to bother him too much, but I was able to talk to him for a short while. I hope he knows how much he has helped me and others like me.

Several months after this first UFO conference, Bill asked me if I would like to meet another abductee. I agreed to this meeting, and shortly afterward met Leah Haley.

Leah has recalled many abduction events quite similar to my own. In addition to the experiences with the strange beings, Leah has also recalled several significant incidents—intrusions by military personnel apparently interested in her experiences with the grays.

As Leah related her experiences with the military to me, I began to feel very uneasy. The things she told me were very disturbing. I began to think of my own experiences with persons connected to the military and wondered what real connection our government has with the strange beings who have become a part of our lives.

I knew Leah was having some difficulty dealing with her recently uncovered memories, and I didn't know if anything I could say would help ease her mind. I shared some of my experiences, and we found many similarities concerning our visitations. I found that Leah was also beginning to receive telepathic communications that paralleled the vernacular of the messages I had received. They seemed very alike in style and the usage of words. This "style" is very different from the way either Leah or I speak or write. It was very unusual.

This first meeting with Leah ended as I had to return home because of previous commitments. We said our good-byes, knowing we would see each other again and continue our communication.

The next morning after our visit, my roommate discovered that a personal object had been removed from the glove compartment of my car and placed on the barbecue pit next to our front door. When we inspected my car, we noticed the glove compartment open and papers strewn about as if someone had been looking for something. It was very eerie.

Soon afterward, several other objects disappeared from my home. One of these was a large crystal, which subsequently reappeared in the seat of my roommate car while he was at work. This crystal had not been in the seat when the car had been parked. This happened on the same day that my roommate had been contacted by someone claiming to be a military person who had some knowledge of UFO phenomena.

I did not know what to think of these happenings, but I began to feel watched. I told Leah about this, and we both agreed that it was significant. I have not had many contacts with supposed military personnel concerning my abduction experiences, but little intrusions and odd happenings do always seem to let me know someone is keeping an eye on me. These incidents happen about twice a year.

In the last few years, I have had several opportunities to meet other abductees, and it always helps us to know we are not alone with our strange experiences. One of the best things to come from talking of my experiences is the fact that I have met many new friends—abductees and researchers who are all searching for answers to this mystery. So many wonderful, intelligent people out there are trying to find out the truth about what is happening on this planet. I feel blessed with these new friendships. It makes me feel less alone in my quest for understanding.

Chapter 17
Communication Breakdown

In the past five years I have run through a river of emotions concerning my UFO experiences. It is difficult to explain how I feel about our alien visitors. I love them at times, but sometimes I get so angry I could wring their scrawny necks.

They have changed my understanding of reality. I will never see the world through sheltered eyes again. I feel that I am a better human being than I was before I was aware of these experiences. I feel stronger. I feel that my strength has come from within—from some primitive survival instinct. Strength through adversity may be the most positive aspect of this experience.

In the spring of 1992 I began working on a series of telepathic messages that had been given to me to give to the public. I was a human fax machine.

When receiving these "communications," I often felt an emotional tone or response to the information. I could feel the spirit or emotion of the sender. I could sense a confrontational tone. On the other hand, some of the entries seemed very positive and spiritual. Perhaps I was not supposed to understand, but simply pass the words along.

Why was I given this information? If the visitors disapprove of the government, maybe they should tell a Congressman and leave me alone. Maybe they were just trying to evoke an emotional response from me. I have no real understanding of this part of myself and my connection to the Source. When I began this journal, I agreed to share the information with the rest of the population. The following entries were dictated to me during that period. This is what they wanted you to know:

October 20, 1991

We are the communicators who have been designated to share information critical to the understanding and survival of your planet. We have grown impatient with the continued suppression of information concerning the awareness of life on other worlds and the interaction with your population. The egocentric nature of man is short-sighted in its acceptance of other intelligent life forms.

You are a seeded planet, a colonized world. In its primitive state, Earth was cultivated with genetic boosters grafted into the existing population. Human existence has been carefully maintained and observed by the Guardians. Much of your folklore and religious beliefs have come from appearances of these Guardians.

At selected times there have been supervised alterations in the continued evolution of the human species. These alterations are comprised of genetic grafting into the existing populace—DNA codes that strengthen the species and increase intelligence capabilities.

You are now reaching a time of great change. The majority of your people have matured to the level of acceptance. You are capable of understanding your heritage. A percentage of the populace are being tutored for the transition period to come.

Many humans will resist change and rebuke the inevitable. The tutored subjects will become helpers during transition. The helpers have been chosen for their strength in adversity. They will be beleaguered with negativity and resistance. Blame will rest unfairly on their shoulders. The helpers are chosen from a cross-section of the overall population. The tribal governments will cease to exist. In their place will be the new world federation—a governing body which will maintain order, and whose members will regulate and supervise relations with your interplanetary neighbors. The federation will be formed to lessen confusion in more primitive areas of the Earth.

At present there are governments within governments—a circle of power with virtually unlimited financial resources and questionable motives. We have had dealings with these secretive conspirators. Mutual distrust and misunderstandings prevail. In the days ahead there will be a face-to-face engagement between the differing parties, and a settlement will be agreed upon. Until that time, your peoples' eyes will be covered by the veil of secrecy. Truth prevails and reality cannot be restrained forever.

October 23, 1991

The condition of your planet is disturbing to us. You seem not to understand the delicacy of the life-giving ecosystems. Your people thrive on self-centered activities that damage the living conditions of all creatures of Earth. It is time to wake up. All are endangered. Now is the time to change the greedy behaviors. You cannot continue as if the Earth is yours. It is not. It was given to you in trust. You were placed upon the planet as seedlings. You have overgrown its boundaries and forgotten your purpose. Each species of plant and animal is intricately dependent on each other. Earth is a tapestry of life. All life is con-

nected and valued. The loss of ozone will continue to damage the species by ultraviolet radiation. The quality of breathable atmosphere will diminish as vegetation is destroyed. It is a dangerous cycle of destruction. For those remaining upon the planet, life will be difficult at best. The transplantation of species to other worlds will lessen the stress on Earth. However, there must be intensive revitalization and conservation to reverse the current threatening conditions.

October 24, 1991

We will give you a limited description of what we are and how we are connected. We are a biological species capable of transmogrification from physical to what you might term spiritual. We do not leave our bodies, but transform them. We can appear differently to each individual witness. What appears to one may not appear to the next. We critically evaluate the mental capacity of those we visit. It is necessary to understand. Your human form can be quite frightening to other species. What is beautiful or grotesque is programmed conditioning, different in each species. Some beings do not relate to visual appearance, but react to smell or auditory frequencies. We evaluate the diversity. We also research the emotional response when there is a reaction to stimuli.

October 25, 1991

In the last 50 of your years, we have increased observance of your people. The increase in the technological skills was of great interest to us. The onslaught of nuclear capabilities and production of weapons of mass destruction was a subject of great concern. The frivolous use of this technology was a precedent that endangered life on the planet and beyond. We began an intensive study of all installations with such dangerous developments. Your technology exceeded your mental capacity of sensible applications. In some instances we were compelled to intervene. Your scientists were seemingly unaware that continued nuclear blasting could rupture the planet and damage the equilibrium of the natural rotation.

As you began to develop the technology to leave the planet, we decided it was time to prepare you for life beyond your realm of existence. The universe is to be shared, not conquered. You are not the superior beings you make yourselves out to be. Superiority comes from benign coexistence, not barbaric takeovers. Our appearance was met with military defensive posturing before we were allowed to explain our presence. All attempts to show ourselves were perceived as a threatening invasion. We were simply targets for the military. At this point we began covert action. We began a study of the general population. This includes immobilization and research. This is necessary to keep you from any threatening action. Once a subject is capable of rational behavior, immobilization is released and dialogue can begin.

Some of your people will misunderstand. You must realize we were attacked. For us to continue and complete our mission of indoctrination, we proceeded in this fashion. Consider your relationships with other species on your planet. If the dog bites, the dog is restrained and domesticated. You take a pup and befriend it before it learns negative behaviors. It is similar in many ways to our actions.

We begin indoctrination with your children before they learn to hate. These children, as adults, will enable us to coexist in mutually beneficial roles. It is a slow process that is coming of age.

November 7, 1991

A time of great change will soon occur on your planet. A League of Controllers orchestrate conditions of rule upon your people. They are secretive and sly in their actions. This group is manipulating the consciousness of your society into submissiveness. One method is the repetitive frequencies bombarding the airwaves around you. It is a subtle conditioning of the population. The majority of your people do not think for themselves. They are told what to buy, what to believe in, and how to behave in order to fit in with society. All of this conditioning is based on false images.

Your nation is becoming a nation of sheep. Free thinking is dangerous to the Controllers. The financially secure are the easiest to condition. The desire for the latest technological gadgetry is the concept that makes the society most vulnerable. The children are also targeted. They are weakened by their addiction to recreational technology, both physically and intellectually.

Consider this: In the event of a complete electromechanical shutdown, the status quo will be in utter chaos. The "have nots" will be least affected because of their survival skills. Become aware of your addiction to electricity. Wean yourself from it. Train for the times ahead. Observe the world around you. Become strong in mind and body. Do not buy into the false security being fed to you daily. Be prepared.

November 10, 1991

We are amused with the short-sighted attempts to look for life elsewhere in the universe. The SETI program is merely a placebo—a system put into place to soften the standard consciousness of the unbelieving and cover the tracks of those who know and choose secrecy.

Your scientists look with narrow vision. They do not understand the wide scope of diversity. There is life that thrives on a nitrogen-methane based atmosphere. Your people would not recognize it as life, but as an atmospheric aberration. You expect all life to be formed as you are, and to communicate in similar fashion. This is not the most consistent design in the universe. Your species has not matured enough to understand the great diversity. You are petty in your knowledge—spoiled children who vie for supremacy. You are children with dangerous toys. There is hope for you. Many are becoming spiritually mature. Many are growing to understand their place in the universal family. This knowledge is an awakening of your inner selves to all that is truth. With this truth comes responsiblity.

December 4, 1991

An interdimensional shift of emerging time lines is coming into focus. Openings of specific dimensional doorways will allow passage of physically attuned/spiritually prepared individuals. Signs of this rare occurrence are appearing for those sensitive enough to respond. A revitalization of human consciousness is occurring as the time for emergence nears.

A percentage of human participants are being prepared on a subconscious level to merge with your sister dimension for an exchange of understanding. There is an acceleration of the higher consciousness of approximately 35% of the Earth's population for adaptation. Windows to universal interdimensional existence will begin to appear in the coming year of 1992. This opportunity will be avail-

able for several years and will then close. This will be the last occurrence of its kind for this age and this planet. The gnosis revealed by the select will be ignored by many. For those aware of the coming event, all input should be evaluated for specific emphasis.

December 12, 1991

The process of opening up the powers of your mind is a many-layered interest. Once you are triggered for awakening, you begin a chain reaction of events that influences all aspects of life around you. By becoming aware of your connection to all life in the universe, you become more considerate to all. Your connection makes you more protective of the world around you.

All actions taken against others are self-destructive. By preserving and protecting other species, you increase your chance of survival. Life given to Earth is interconnecting. View all life forms as cells in the body of Earth's life force. It is a mirror to the soul of man.

As man becomes corrupt and uncaring, the corruption is reflected in the destruction of life upon your planet. Your world is nearing the point of destruction. It is a cancer on the body of Earth; it spreads rapidly. Indifference and greed are suicidal traits killing your world. By involving ourselves in your lives, we make you aware of your connection to lesser life forms.

We are amused by the indignation response of those we have researched. The rantings of personal rights being violated, as we do the physical examinations, are amusing as well. By the forced participation in our research, you become aware of your connection to all life forms. Those with the advanced awareness withstand the exams and understand the need for them. Those who participate and respond with curiosity are then tutored for the future. Those who hate us and fear us for what we do are not capable of understanding the life connection. Make note: You eradicate species on your planet with no thought as to their choice to be destroyed. You take far more from them than we take from you.

If steps are not taken to stop the destruction of life on your planet, the Guardians will assume the responsibility. The choice is up to you. Free will is allowed only if such actions do not become self-destructive. Personal rights become negated when the result is destruction. We prefer to give you the choice. However, the majority of governing bodies are ruled by greed and corruption. Survival of your planet may depend upon insurrection.

If intervention is deemed necessary, it will be seen as an invasion force by the greater percentage of the population. At this time, those individuals whom we have tutored and studied will assume supervisory roles and will intercede on our behalf. They will assist us in creating a survivable environment for all the inhabitants of Earth.

December 22, 1991

This season you call Christmas was once a time of good will toward others in respect of the birth of the Exalted One. It was a time to consider the connection between all members of your planet. The meaning of this time is changing to a season of greed. The hunger for more possessions has perverted the original concept. You are subliminally programmed to believe the true measure of love is to provide the most objects to your circle of significant ones.

For those showered with gifts, there is no understanding of true joy. Because of your connection with all life, the sorrow of others will affect your inner self. There is no true joy when others hunger for the simplest necessities.

Many will never realize this aspect of Christmas. How many of you would forfeit all gifts to your significants in order to feed a hungry stranger? Therein lies true joy.

Each year the chasm between the prosperous and the needy widens. This is no accident. It is a means of control. The prosperous are slaves to their greed and placated by their material objects. The needy are shunned by others and distracted by their survival efforts. The Controllers have used this method of power to keep you lethargic. Only when you awaken to your inner knowledge, do you become able to break free.

This awakening is occurring at a faster rate. Many can now see the deceptions. By recognizing your connection to others, you are linking together. Many will never reach this level. They are the sheep. They are spiritual infants who cannot be forced into awareness. These sheep will continue as they always have, living their lives blindly with no understanding. It is not their time. Do not concern yourself with them.

You must begin linking with others who are psychically aligned to your level of awareness. It is your duty and purpose to create the change necessary to break free of the power brokers who control your people. Be aware that your understanding makes you dangerous. The Controllers want to rule your planet. A power play of great proportions is occurring. It will not succeed. It will be a difficult time for everyone.

The awakening is in full force. It is time to come together as one united consciousness. Prepare yourself for the difficult path facing you. It is important that these writings be made available to those who will understand. Do not allow yourself to be censored. The Agency of Deceit is worried about disclosure threatening their way of life. Be cautious. Attune yourself to your intuition; it will not betray you. It is more accurate than you realize.

December 30, 1991

The gateways are opening at strategic locations across the planet's surface. Many changes will occur. The Stonehenge port is the primary entrance location to the parallax dimension. Other windows with fluctuating pathways are soon to develop. These include Teotihuacan, Easter Island, and the Rock of Presidents. Be alert to anomalous displays.

December 31, 1991

Prepare for the beginning of the change of consciousness of higher life forms. Now begins an upward path to harmonious connections of universal intellect. Be also prepared for upheaval, as change will not come easily. The changes of the past year will continue and multiply to the coming year and beyond. Be strong and forthright in your beliefs. Prepare for outward signs of change. We will be seen by many. The population must face reality. We are with you. More will come to know us. Earth faces a difficult time, but the end result will be a positive one.

January 10, 1992

The advances gained from counter-evolutionary advocates are of a limited nature. The DNA complex can be traced to prove the responsive element of species adaptation and development over a span of time. There must be a cohesive blending of science and spirit to maximize knowledge concerning the development of the universe.

March 10, 1992

Your world is ruled by the invisible government. Currency is their country, greed and power their gods of choice. Strategic Defense Initiative is locking your world away from outside assistance. It is a wolf in sheep's clothing. Your weapons face outward. Confrontation is inevitable; prepare for it. Difficult choices must be made. The fate of your planet balances precariously on the decision.

March 28, 1992

Realize this above all else; the life systems of Earth are severely out of balance. Nothing less than social revolution on a worldwide scale can save this planet from becoming a toxic wasteland. Change must occur. Token concessions from the greedy industrialists and self-serving Controllers are not sufficient. You do not have 20 years to make these decisions. Open your eyes to what is ahead. Planetary preservation must be the priority. All other considerations are insignificant. You have been warned. The consequences will be of your own design.

April 3, 1992

The evolving soul of man is absorbing the essence of all life throughout the universe. The developed consciousness can tap into many aspects of existence beyond the flimsy curtain of personal realities. This awareness encompasses all of what exists. The good and evil, the amoral and apathetic, are all available to present themselves. All is not good. All is not evil. Each is a part of the whole of existence.

The evolving consciousness opens your eyes to realities

that have always been with you. You, only now, are able to see and understand. Learn to focus inward, as well as outward, to understand the meaning of who you are and your purpose of being.

April 8, 1992

It is time for the world to make its changes. We are being forced to accelerate actions against the agencies that have repeatedly demonstrated hostile intent. We cannot allow the threatening weaponry to circle your planet, ready to make war against new, and perhaps unprepared, visitors. Make note of all developments from this point forward. Nothing is by chance or accident.

Occurrences are taking place across the planet in an effort to inspire the Agency of Deceit to cease hostilities. Possible instigations of the easily inflamed tribal nations may provide the excuse for increased defense posturing. It is only a funnel of power to wage the secret war against your planetary neighbors.

Be aware that the current leaders of your secret government will do anything to stay in power and keep those of like mind in power. They live in a state of fear that borders on panic. They see their secret world fraying at the edges. They will lose their secret soon. It is beyond their control.

There came a time when I realized I had to stop writing this information. I began to see these beings in a different light. I think I reached a point at which they no longer needed to whitewash everything. I saw too many "what ifs" on the horizon. I was disturbed by the amount of control these visitors possessed. They can take me or anyone when they want, and I cannot stop them. They have the upper hand, and I am in no position to change that fact. It is a very sickening sensation to be aware of one's helplessness.

I have heard it said that the reason the government has kept these experiences secret is because they do not want to admit they have no control over the situation. They don't think the public can handle it. I agree that it is a difficult situation. It is hard to accept the fact that another civilization is intruding into our lives. It is harder to accept that we may be considered only cattle or "little pet humans."

I have survived this knowledge. I survived the abductions; I have survived the silence. In order to maintain public calm, people like me are treated as jokes. We are doubly damned. We are scapegoats and targets for ridicule. From my point of view, something is very wrong with this picture. I don't trust the aliens, and I don't trust the government. I only trust in myself and God.

I didn't always feel this way. At the point that I quit writing these "dictated" messages, I went through a phase of terrible aloneness. It was a very dark time for me. I didn't realize it, but this was the beginning of my "fear year." It was a period of my life that is very painful to remember or discuss. I have decided to share this information with others—not to dwell on the negative side, but to demonstrate that it is possible to rise above the fear to become a stronger, wiser person.

Chapter 18
The Dark Side

After the first hypnosis session uncovered my personal involvement with alien beings, my primary emotion was awe. I was overwhelmed by the enormity of what had occurred. I had actually been contacted, prodded, and experimented on by another humanoid species. It was too much to grasp.

My whole understanding of myself in relation to my environment evaporated. How could I have made contact with an alien race? And why? It seemed an event of global proportions. I felt at a loss. What should I do with this information? Other people continued their every-day routines while I struggled secretly with the experience.

I was no longer an Ozarker or a Missourian—or an American. I was now an Earthling. All my troubles, problems, and concerns were insignificant compared to the bigger universal picture. The wars and confrontations of hostile nations now seemed like trivial neighborhood spats.

As more hypnosis revealed a lifetime of alien contact, I thought I understood my visitors. The grays indicated that they were taking humans for "mutually beneficial" research. I was told that the eggs and sperm taken from humans were being "grafted" with alien genetics in order to evolve both species. I was told that we were being studied, and that we would need their help to prevent the destruction of Earth. This seemed fine and good; I could learn to forget the pain and trauma inflicted on me if many were to benefit. I felt I had both the ability and the duty to make a sacrifice that would save my own kind and help a race of extraterrestrials as well. I was a regular Jeanne of Arc!

That state of mind lasted about three years. Then in 1992, I began to question my attitude. I was on good terms with the grays, and they were giving me telepathic information I could share with others. The telepathic connection was keeping me informed about almost any subject I cared to explore. It occurred to me that I was much too agreeable.

As I met more "abductees," we began to compare our experiences. All of us were being told the same things. We were "special." We were helping another species survive. Together we could save the planet. Our children were being taken to a wonderful garden colony for a new beginning. We had been chosen for this honorable duty. The most dangerous statement I heard was "they know what's best for us."

The more I heard, the more I felt we all were being fed a line of garden manure. It was as if a lover had told me wonderful, sweet things to make me feel special, and then I discovered, while talking to friends, that he had told them the same old lines. The words lose their "special" quality. Are they true, or just lies to keep us complacent?

I became overwhelmed by "What ifs." What if it were all lies? What if the aliens' motives were malevolent? I "What iffed" myself into a state of fear and paranoia that lasted a year and a half. I call it my "fear year."

In 1991 and early 1992, I kept an "alien journal" of dictated messages that were to be presented to the public. I became more and more engrossed in the process of receiving this information. It became harder and harder to remain objective about the information. I began to have emotional reactions to the contents of the messages I received.

The messages spoke of a "secret government" and the control this group had on the world population. As I wrote all the information down, I became increasingly distressed. It was beginning to sound very subversive. I was out of the military by this time, but I still felt some sort of patriotic connection to the government.

I became worried that this anti-government rhetoric would get me in trouble. I voiced my worries to several friends. They read the messages that bothered me but did not see any reason for me to worry. They didn't think the information contained anything out of the ordinary mistrust of government that many people were feeling.

I continued to write the information down whenever I felt the "nudge." Again I began to have strong reactions to the information. Yet, nothing I had recorded would account for these strong worries of subversion that I was feeling. A thought occurred to me: Was I receiving some kind of subliminal information at the same time that I was receiving the messages for the general public?

I started becoming withdrawn from the world around me. I felt strange and different from everyone I knew. I continued to record the dictated information, and I began to receive visual images along with the words. In my mind's eye, I saw people taking over buildings and blowing up power stations. Suddenly I had enough. I thought, "No! I don't have to go along with this!" As soon as I relayed that thought, I received the reply, "*WE KNOW WHAT SCARES YOU*." At that point, I received a visual image of a reptilian being sexually aggressive with a child.

This was an image I had seen before.

It was during an abduction in 1990. I had gone to visit friends who had been having sightings and incidents almost nightly. A friend and I visited them one night to see if anything might happen. I had been having mostly positive experiences at that time and wanted to see these beings again. I wanted to learn more. My friends were having some negative experiences, but I thought they weren't as experienced as I was in these matters. I was very wrong.

During the night, after a barbecue and good conversation, we sat outside, watching the stars. At some point in time, we seemed to move into some type of altered state. We began to pair off, and the atmosphere turned very sexual. It was sexual, but very mechanical in nature—as if we were running through all the complexities of human sexuality minus the emotion.

Most of what happened that night was hidden in my subconscious—erased from memory. I later asked for a hypnosis session to try to recall the missing memories. At some time after the sexual events, the grays appeared, and we were all led outside and into a craft. I was separated from the rest of the group. I was unaware of what the others experienced during this separation.

A gray led me into a room that was empty except for a table. There was a small window on one wall. I stood in this room and waited. Soon a gray came into the room with one of the reptilian creatures. I was told, telepathically, that I was supposed to have sex with this creature. I rebelled instantly, thinking strongly, "No! No! No!" I was then taken out of the room. The creatures seemed much too agreeable.

I was taken to another room next to the room I had just left. I could see the reptilian through a small window in the wall. There was a gray standing with me, as I looked into the next room. I saw a door open up into the other room that held the reptilian.

I watched in horror as a child was led into this room with the reptile! I had the immediate telepathic understanding that, since I had refused to be with this creature, the child was to take my place! I cannot describe the feeling that I experienced at that moment. I came unglued. I felt sick, helpless, horrified, and frightened beyond belief. I also felt the most intense anger I had ever known. I reacted with the animal response of a mother protecting her young. It was primitive and it was ugly and it came from a part of me that I didn't know existed.

I went for the throat of the gray that stood next to me. I was going to choke the creature or rip it to shreds! I never made contact with the gray. A beam of light came from the hand of the gray standing with me. It hit me across the ribcage. It felt like a bolt of electricity.

Just as I lost consciousness, I saw the image of the reptilian and the child disappear. It seemed to be only a holographic image they had used to create this response in me. They had, indeed, uncovered my deepest fear. I could withstand almost anything, but the threat of such horror to an innocent child or others whom I love was my weak spot.

The next morning, everyone awoke full of anxiety. The five of us remembered bits and pieces, but most of what happened lay hidden in our minds. We didn't fully realize what had happened until we distanced ourselves from each other. It wasn't until later the next day that the strangeness of the evening became apparent.

I was seized with an intense need to hurry home. I wanted to see if my family was okay. I didn't know why, but I was extremely worried. I had no apparent reason to worry, but I had to assure myself that everyone was okay. Everything seemed normal, except for my strong sense of fear and the desire to protect those I care about. I felt the need to take a shower, and when I undressed, I noticed a wide bruise across my ribcage that I could not explain.

I was an emotional wreck for almost a month after this encounter. All those who were involved in this experience were deeply affected by it. The incident created a distance between us and damaged a blossoming friendship. The fear of a repetition of that night keeps us apart.

I do not know what this change of events meant for me. I can only say that I did not recognize any of the creatures who appeared that night. It seemed to be a different group—one whose motives seemed much more sinister. I realized that many facets of the abduction experience were unknown to me.

The image of the child and the reptilian was flashed into my mind two years later as I tried to assert myself concerning my feelings about the aliens' anti-government concepts. They did, indeed, know my deepest fears and did not hesitate to remind me of this. I felt frightened and helpless, but I let them know I would not be a part of any violent rebellion. I remember that, at some point, they let me know it wouldn't be necessary because plenty of people were available who were not as squeamish as I about such things.

I had telepathic arguments with the Source of these communications. I voiced my opinions that I was an American, who had God-given rights to my freedoms and that was what this country was founded on. The answer I received to that tirade chilled me to the bone. I was asked, "*Why are you so loyal to a government who traded your life and the lives of your children for a handful of computer chips?"*

This event began my spiral down into the deepest depression I have ever known. I trusted no one. I refused to write down any more communications. I felt that the automatic writing gave the Source too much control over my mind. I tried to tell people what was happening to me, but I didn't feel that they understood. When I tried to explain further, I felt I was only causing them to fear me. I was voicing fears no one wanted to think about.

I felt out of control. I worried about what these creatures could make me do. Would they make me do something that I felt was morally wrong? Images from fifties B-movies haunted me. Were we becoming "pod people"? I imagined frightening images of people being held down and given implants, of the entire population of the planet under control of the visitors.

I tried to find relief at abductee support-group meetings. Everyone seemed to be having such positive experiences that I was like a black cloud descending over the group. One lady told me I should think more positively because my negativity might spread to others. Or maybe it was PMS or early menopause. Any explanation except for the obvious one: there are some bad entities out there.

I began to feel like a pariah. I knew there was no way I could explain the intensity of my fear to anyone who hadn't experienced it. I avoided my abductee friends because the lady had been right. I did have an atmosphere of darkness around me that affected everyone I came into contact with. I could not force myself to think positively because I saw only darkness on my horizon.

I continued to isolate myself more and more. I began to drink heavily to forget the pain I was in. It only made me sicker the next day. I didn't do anything but go to work, come home, cook supper, and go to sleep. My daughter didn't understand what was happening to me and began to act out in her own way. I would go days without bathing or cleaning the house. I was a pathetic excuse for a human being.

I thought of everything I had experienced and been told. Was it all true? I couldn't trust the aliens, and I didn't really trust the government. When I expressed my concerns about receiving such negative telepathic information, someone told me there were indications that our government could receive and transmit information in the same manner as the aliens. I had to consider that my own government might be bombarding me with negativity in order to change my attitude about the abductions. Now I was really confused. I felt threatened from all sides.

I grew tired of fighting such an intense mental battle. I couldn't tell the general public what was out there or what was happening. I was struggling to survive. I felt so alone! I had to keep a normal countenance at work to keep food on the table. I was barely making it and felt I was losing ground fast.

I decided I was going to write the President a letter! Clinton had just been elected, and he seemed more approachable than any of the others in recent years. I had to tell someone what was happening to me. I was a citizen, and I wanted protection. Either that, or I just wanted someone to admit that they were aware of the problem and were trying to find a solution.

I worked on it for about a week before I mailed it. I felt a feverish need to get it written because I had to mail it soon. I didn't know why, but I knew I had to get it done. I fine-tuned it until I was satisfied. The following is the meat of the message I sent:

Dear Mr. President,

I am one of those "crazy lunatic" people who have had recollections and indications of what seem to be abductions by alien beings. I know this sounds like I am a crackpot, but I hope you will give me an honest listen.

I don't know why this is happening to me and many others. I don't know what it is that is occurring. I just know I'm having some unusual experiences I cannot control. I've done my best to learn and understand and still maintain my sanity. It isn't easy. I am afraid for myself, my family, and humanity in general. Some have said there is a great amount of government secrecy concerning the subject of UFOs and alien contact.

I can understand this, considering the tremendous effect

on the social order of man. The fact that other intelligent life forms are interacting and experimenting with our population is unsettling. Not knowing the motives behind these occurrences is frightening.

My own experiences have been both positive and negative. On the up side, I have gained an appreciation of Earth's environment and a connection with all life therein. On the other hand, it has been horrific and painful. The hardest thing to bear is the loss of control over my life. I cannot stop this from happening to myself or my children. I have a support group, researchers, and a few friends and family members to confide in. This provides some help to me, but I'm still alone when I face the night.

I make no claims of being a model citizen. My life has been tumultuous. However, I try to learn from my mistakes. I do my best to treat everyone fairly. I served my country for a while. This includes two years spent in the Arkansas National Guard...

Lately, I have felt an increase in these anomalous disturbances. Something is happening. I feel sort of locked into a type of superconsciousness. I know that sounds bizarre. It is getting harder to conceal the stress while I attempt to lead a normal life. I work 40 hours a week for a fraction above minimum wage. It is a struggle to keep my family afloat in these tough economic times.

Thousands of us are experiencing this phenomenon in varying degrees. We aren't all crazy. Many people from all walks of life are reporting these incidents. If the US government knows anything about this, we should be told. I need to know what I'm up against. Shouldn't there at least be a government study done on the psychological aftermath? I would gladly share any information I have gained from a lifetime of intrusions, if the American people would benefit.

Many countries and governments now accept the existence of UFOs. Yet, in my country, we are silenced by ridicule. We are struggling to survive trauma that would make some catatonic, yet we are treated as jokes. Mine is only one of many voices. I feel I must speak out about this. Somebody has to. I do not know who will read this. I do not know what the consequences of my writing this letter will be. I only know I feel a tremendous urgency to do so. I believe in my country and my people. The American people should be told the truth if anyone knows what is happening here—even if the answer creates a sociological dilemma....

I finished the letter and mailed it. When I returned from the post office, I turned on the television. A special report said someone had just bombed the World Trade Center. My throat tightened. I couldn't breathe! I had just mailed a weird letter to the president about UFOs, and now this had to happen! I watched the coverage of rescue efforts on TV as the realization of terrorism in the United States struck me with deep sadness.

Two nights later, another news report told of David Koresh and a hundred or so followers holed up in a compound in Waco, Texas. As I watched the events unfold, a strong feeling overcame me. "He's felt the Influence and thinks it's God!" I felt a sinking feeling in my stomach as I considered the possibilities. The world around me seemed to be falling apart. And my own future looked infinitely darker.

Chapter 19
Rebirth

In the spring of 1993, I continued to sink into a growing sense of despair. Everything around me was falling apart. My home life was full of tension and stress. I was living in a small city, and my neighborhood was full of crime and shady people.

My daughter was suffering from the effects of my depression as well as from the influences of the city streets. Her behavior became more and more erratic.

In addition to the things happening around us, I feel there were several more abductions that caused everything to come to a climax at that time.

My health began to suffer. I had numerous physical symptoms of illness but didn't know what kind. I began to visit a doctor. I spent several hundred dollars without success. At one point, I told him I had been depressed for quite some time. He prescribed anti-depressants and told me to come back if my problems continued.

The pills lessened the physical responses of depression. I realized

I had been clinically depressed for years and had become physically ill as a result. After two weeks of taking the pills, I began to function better, but I was still scared of my own shadow.

In April, several incidents occurred that made me decide to leave the city. My daughter was having trouble in school, and her behavior got out of hand. She began "hanging out" with some rough kids in the neighborhood. The stresses of the city got to be too much.

I packed up everything and moved back to the country. I left my job, my house, and the three-year-long relationship I was in. I felt I had lost everything I had ever cared about, and I didn't think I could get any lower than how I was feeling at that moment. But it was probably the best thing I could have done. I had to start all over with everything, but I knew it was the right move. As I was thinking about what to do, I heard a small voice telling me I would be okay. The voice told me that I was a spiritual being who could transcend the negativity I was feeling.

I began to see images. Concepts came to me in the same way as the telepathic communications, but accompanied by a feeling of safety. I saw myself as a creature of light and energy. My body was merely a cocoon that I would someday shed. I felt that all the fear I had lived with for so long was a test.

I knew that bad things would happen as well as good, and that I must be ready to withstand changes that lay ahead. Beings of light existed at a higher level than the alien beings I had encountered. These spiritual beings would always be there for me as long as I believed they were there for me. I had only to acknowledge their existence to receive their help.

I began to equate this voice with the God I had known since childhood. This felt like the God I had believed in throughout my life. I had abandoned my religion because of the restrictions and the images of a God of fear and retribution. Those images never fit with the God who I felt loved all creatures, despite their diversity and mistakes.

I reacquainted myself with the Creator of the universe and the angels of light who guide us. I began to pray again, in a way that felt comfortable for me—not restricted by any previous belief system. I asked for help, understanding, and protection.

The change in me began almost immediately. I first had to recognize myself as a spirit and not a physical creature. I had to quit worrying about the physical world and concern myself with the growth of the spirit. I had to come to the realization that, when my body dies, I will still exist. All that matters is knowing in my heart I have done the right things and following what I know in my heart is good.

I learned that good and evil come in many forms. The more one aligns oneself to what one knows is good, the more one will attract positive energy. I was not to pretend that evil creatures do not exist. I had to acknowledge the existence of all the forces of the universe. The laws of the universe consist of balance between positive and negative energies. By praying, I acknowledge my connection with beings of light who can help me rise above negative influences. I just have to reach out for the connection when I am bombarded by fear. Everything that happens in the physical world we live in is a test of our souls.

I feel that a great confrontation between all the creatures who now exist physically is coming. All of us are aware of this within ourselves. Our knowledge transcends all religious and cultural beliefs. The depth of it is beyond my comprehension. I feel it relates to the Christian beliefs of the second coming of Christ and the last days, but in a magnitude that makes the Biblical description seem like a fairy tale.

My "fear year" was a test for me. Maybe it was the ultimate test of my soul. Soon after it ended, the fear and anxiety lifted off my shoulders and I started to get healthier and happier. I still get scared, but I know that, whatever happens, I can withstand it with help and faith. I can't do it all on my own. I had to break through the barrier that religion had created in my mind in order to find God.

Chapter 20
On the Edge of the Future

Writing this book has helped me understand my memories and experiences better by forcing me to focus on them. During these last few months, I have had to search my soul for truth. I do not take my responsibility lightly. So many spiritually hungry people are looking for answers...I don't want to lead anyone astray.

My truths are not yours necessarily. My own opinions change rapidly. By the time this appears in print, they may have reversed. Like everyone else, I am searching. I may never find the answers to all my questions.

The telepathic communications intrigue me. I want to keep that communication link open, but I don't want to risk my soul to do so. Several sources have warned me to protect myself when I allow the words to flow through me, lest any manner of spirit enter my thoughts.

Several years ago, I became frightened and stopped the communications. Then I began to feel that it is important to explore this part of myself. I began to read spiritual books of all types and all religions.

I began to read the Bible like never before. Whenever I found a truth that I recognized in my heart, I would save it in my memory.

Several verses in the Bible seemed to speak to me concerning the communications:

> If you call me I will answer you, and tell you great and mysterious things, which you do not understand. (Jeremiah 33:3, NEB)

I knew I could learn many things through these experiences, but I wanted to be sure the sender was a good and proper source. I certainly did not want to contact anything evil. My continued search for answers in the Bible yielded this verse:

> Do not trust any and every spirit, my friends, test the spirits, to see whether they are from God, for among those who have gone out into the world there are many prophets falsely inspired. This is how we may recognize the Spirit of God: every spirit which acknowledges that Jesus Christ has come in the flesh is of God. (1 John 4:1-2, NEB)

This seemed like a perfect way to protect myself. It was the closest thing to a guarantee I could find. Shortly thereafter, when I found myself home alone on a very quiet evening, I experimented with this theory. I said a short prayer. "Lord, allow me to receive any necessary information, but only through the spirits of Jesus Christ, our Savior." I wanted to be completely sure I had covered all bases.

The answer I received came in several segments:

December 28, 1994, 7:00 PM

> *The day is come when many false prophets speak of wonders of which none has ever seen. The fruit of their labor is pleasing to the eye, poison to the soul.*

This seemed somewhat choppy and hard to understand. I was not sure what I was being told. I waited a moment and the thoughts continued:

Jesus, our Father, speak to us today in the hour of our need.

This seemed very odd. It was like a Catholic prayer. I was raised a Baptist, and this was not how I pray. It was as if I had contacted some sort of spiritual middleman, who in turn contacted someone else. It continued:

Three signs will I give you for the Day of Reckoning:

1. The clouds and wind will come forth and destroy many who are not prepared for these happenings. The power of mighty winds shall be unleashed from all quarters. Many dwellings shall be washed away and destroyed, and lives will be lost in the maelstrom. As the days warm the earth, prepare for the first sign.

This seemed to be speaking of hurricanes and other violent weather phenomena. That was the visual image I received. It continued:

2. The earth will vomit fire upon the lands, destruction in many places, but the greatest terror will come from the Great Veil that covers the sun's face. Darkness will cover the earth for many days. The fire comes from within, after the shaking of the earth begins. The seven times seven will bring forth the sign of fire.

This was starting to get spooky. The visual and symbolic images were of volcanic eruptions. The volcanic activity would happen after a series of earthquakes. I felt that the seven times seven was seven earthquakes of a magnitude of seven on the Richter scale. I don't know if it was counting all earthquakes of a seven or greater. The words concluded with the following:

> *3. The souls are gathered on the face of the land for the Great Battle. The souls of light will unite as one. Together in thought, the Light Horse rides into battle. The greatest power lies in the multitude of One. The soulless ones, the face of darkness, prey upon the individual. All of God's true children must come to the light of One and see themselves as the family of God. All who remain have now recognized their alignment. Light and Dark at the Equinox.*
>
> *Many lights pierce the darkness, the sign of three; the final test will come to be.*

I felt very unnerved when this finished. There were no brilliant lights or angelic voices, but I felt I had been told something very significant. This message seemed very apocalyptic. There were plenty of visual images.

The "Great Battle" seemed to be some battle between good and evil. I felt that "souls of light" referred to all those persons who were positive and on the good side. The message seemed to be telling me that all those good persons were uniting in consciousness. I felt this was very necessary for the times ahead. This "united consciousness" was the "Light Horse." It seemed that all the children of God (i.e., positive supreme being) were going to have to put aside their religious differences to battle the powers of evil.

I felt "Light and Dark at the Equinox" was a time frame, or else the souls of good and evil were equal in number. "Many lights pierce the darkness" was possibly the triumph of good over evil. It also could mean a night full of UFO sightings. The sign of three may appear symbolically, perhaps in a crop formation.

I felt it was important to include this message in the book. I have always hated and avoided making personal predictions. I did not want to risk appearing stupid when nothing happened. I do not feel that way about this particular message. I did everything possible to assure it was from a good source. If I disbelieve it, I have to disbelieve Christ. I am unable to do that.

I don't know if this message has anything to do with the aliens. I felt strong references to good and evil, but no inclinations as to who was who. I hesitate to label the grays or any other creature "good" or "bad." I don't know enough yet. Maybe these creatures are simply preparing to watch the coming changes on our world. I plan to stay alert and keep an open mind.

I still feel in a befuddled state of religion. I feel strongly connected to Native American spirituality and various other beliefs. I am part of all life that exists in this universe. When it is time for me to know, the truths will be there for me to find. I will continue to gather knowledge from all sources. I believe God will understand.

Chapter 21
Future Visions, Future Fears

Since I first began writing this book, my feelings about everything have fluctuated through many highs and lows. I have tried to describe everything I have learned from my experiences adequately. There is still so much I don't know.

In 1993, Debbie Jordan and her fiancée opened their home to Erin and me after I made my escape from the city. Their generosity enabled me to get centered and consider what I wanted to do with my life. We had many in-depth discussions of life while downing endless pots of morning coffee.

The time I spent in Indiana was a period of healing for me. The big, sprawling farmhouse was like a sanctuary in the midst of acres of cornfields. Quite a few odd experiences occurred while we were all living there together. My most recent suspected abduction (as of this writing) happened there in late September 1993.

All of us were watching television when Debbie noticed a light in the sky through the window of the front door. We all rushed outside to watch. For a while it remained stationary in the sky above Kokomo. Its glow grew alternately dimmer and brighter. Deb's fiancée scrambled for the video camera and began recording the object. It began moving across the sky in one direction, then reversed course.

When the light moved beyond our viewing range, we remained outside, talking about the incident. My daughter spoke up and said, "Mommy, what's that walking up the road toward us?"

I saw the movement of a tall, lanky creature. I could not quite resolve a definite visual image of its shape. It seemed to be bluish-gray and looked transparent, as if made of smoke. Erin said, "Is it a doggy?" Deb's fiancée said, "It must be some sort of dog." At that point, I had an image in my head of a tall, lanky, long-legged greyhound. I drew a picture of it later that evening.

My memory gets hazy at this point. We were recording all of this on videotape, but never aimed the recorder toward the creature in the road. There was some uneasy laughter about what it could be, then Debbie's fiancée went inside to telephone someone to determine if anyone across town had observed the light. While he was in the house, Debbie and I began to hear beeps coming from the cattle barn.

I had heard this same sound on several other occasions, usually while walking the dogs in the yard at night. Strangely enough, I had never mentioned the sound to anyone before this night. It sounded like an electronic cricket, and I had assumed it was an object associated with an electric fence or something similar. My second assumption was that it was some indigenous Indiana insect. When Debbie mentioned the beeping sound and reacted to it, I realized that it was a noise that did not belong in the area of the cattle barn. I began to get spooked.

Debbie began to record the sound. Each time the beep occurred, she would verbally mark the sound by saying, "There...there...there." I was watching her record the event, making note that the red recording light was the only light I could see other than some street lighting in the area.

After we recorded this sound for several minutes, I felt an uneasiness come over me. I vaguely remember mentioning to Debbie that maybe we should get out of there. At some point, Deb's fiancée came back outside and took the video camera down to the cattle barn in hopes of discovering where the sound was coming from.

Nothing much happened after that, except we saw an object cross the sky in the opposite position from where we had watched the earlier object disappear. It moved too quickly for anyone to record it on video. This light seemed to change from pink to a darker red before it disappeared.

We decided to return to the house and replay the video to see what we had captured on film. We made note as we entered the house that nearly an hour had passed. We had gone outside at 9:50 PM and it was now 11:00. As we watched the video, we realized that the piece of tape Debbie had recorded of the sound was not there! We also noticed that approximately 17 minutes of time was missing from the video compared to the amount of time that we knew we had spent outside.

We felt very strange after that. Debbie and I both feel that something else happened outside that night. Neither of us has explored the event with hypnosis. I have experienced a couple of flashes of memory of the creature walking down the road. It seemed to be bluish-gray and nearly transparent. The most prominent feature of this creature was the long, gangly arms and legs. It walked upright like some type of humanoid, and its legs seemed to hardly touch the ground. I suspect I will look into this event eventually with hypnosis, but I have no driving need to explore it now.

Several months after this event, I returned to Missouri to live. There were more available jobs opening up in the Branson area, and it was time for us to move on. The months I spent with Debbie and her family are very special to me, and I will always be grateful for their hospitality and friendship. They enabled me to sort out my feelings and recuperate from all the upheaval I had experienced during the previous year.

During the next two years after I returned to Missouri, I remembered only a few physical sensations and odd instances that I suspect may be connected to abductions. The year 1995 was unusually quiet for me. It also was a very inactive time for most other experiencers I know. I don't know what to make of this. Have the aliens finished their experiment, or is this the calm before the storm?

While physical instances have subsided, psychogenic activity has increased significantly. I feel that I am experiencing life through other levels of consciousness that are hard for me to interpret. I feel that my mind is much more active and reactive to the world around me than before. I am seeing and feeling life in non-physical ways.

I feel that I am becoming aware of myself as a spiritual being. It is as if my sense of self or my psyche is changing into an ethereal awareness and my physical body is merely a cocoon. I find this difficult to explain to some people. In other instances, I am connecting with individuals who seem to be changing in similar ways. I find these similar souls to be easily recognizable. Whatever it is that is happening is something I see and feel in others and they perceive in me. We are kindred spirits, and we are changing and evolving.

The dark side is still apparent, as well. In April 1995, I became distressed over a disturbing dream I had experienced. In the dream, I was being put through a maze that consisted of many levels of bizarre images in which I had to complete an assigned task in order to move through the levels and finish the "game." This game was monitored by "officials" who were quite human in appearance. These officials were combining computer technology, virtual reality, and LSD. I awoke from this experience extremely distressed.

The days that followed this dream were filled with ever-increasing anxiety. On the third day following the dream, I turned on the television to hear the news of the bombing of the Federal Building in Oklahoma City. I was shocked and sickened by the devastation I was seeing. I felt a sense of fear that the world was out of control and I could do nothing about it.

I watched the rescue efforts and worried about all the people I had known in Oklahoma City when I had lived there many years ago. When I heard the report of the arrest of a suspect, I sensed an eerie similarity between the bombing in Oklahoma City and the earlier bombing of the World Trade Center in New York. In both instances, the suspects were apprehended much more easily and quickly than I would have thought possible. The complexity and magnitude of the bombings did not jibe with the stupidity of the mistakes that caused the suspects to be arrested.

In the days following the incident, I felt the sorrow and fear of the entire nation. I had become aware of my connection to all life, and when this tragedy occurred, I felt the loss in that connection. As Obi Wan Kenobi said in *Star Wars*, I felt "a great disturbance in the force." I began to slip into a depression that nearly rivaled my "fear year."

When I heard that the suspect in the Oklahoma bombing had acted in retaliation for the FBI incident in Waco with David Koresh, my inner warning system sounded an alarm. Once again, I felt a connection to all these different incidents. I knew of no reason for feeling this way, but I wondered if this was a result of the influence of the dark force I did not understand. Now I get chilled to the bone each time I hear the words "Koresh" or "Waco."

I realized in the weeks following the bombing that I had slipped back into the pit of depression and paranoia that I had experienced in 1992. I had to fight off fear and anxiety consciously with prayer and faith in God. I finally had to quit watching television for a time because all the scenes of tragedy and nationwide paranoia were parts of the problem.

My dour mood began to change with the coming of spring. I began to concentrate on the newness of life around me and positive energies instead of negative ones. I read every book I could find on the subject of consciousness and the power of the mind. This was a subject to which I was drawn and the area in which I was experiencing the most growth.

I do not understand my feeling of expanded consciousness, but I know this new depth of perception includes both positive and negative energies. I know I have to strengthen myself because the input I am receiving will intensify. My personality is going to have to expect an increase in information and all the extra emotional feedback that will accompany all the new data.

I realize it is absolutely essential to know exactly who I am as a human being because I will be experiencing the input and emotions of everyone around me. I believe that is why I have been so uncertain and afraid during the times when I sense the Dark Influence is afoot.

I believe I am becoming strongly empathic to the world around me. This empathy touches both the positive and negative energies. If I am to use this ability, I will have to learn to disassociate myself from the feelings that bombard me. The fact that I can feel and sense the darkness does not mean it is a part of me. I feel that by honing this ability I will be able to protect myself and those I care about. I am using this quiet phase of my life to become more assured of who I am. Learning to trust in myself has been a long and difficult lesson for me.

It has been hard to explain the different influences I feel, yet I know I am not the only one to feel the energies surrounding us. I am sure that this frightens people. I am only trying to explain it, understand it, and help others to understand. The whole concept of the power of the mind is greatly misunderstood. It is our thinking that creates who we are. If we disconnect the limitations of the physical body, therein lies the essence of who we are as individuals and as a species.

New and unorthodox thinking often is labeled crazy, evil, or stupid, simply because it deviates from the safe area of "normalcy." We fear what we do not understand. This fear has increased in the last century because of the many changes our species has witnessed. Tightly woven groups of people are desperately trying to hold on to the security blanket of ritualized thinking. To think independently is threatening to those fearful of change. I believe we should challenge our beliefs with independent thought; if a belief has substance, it will withstand change and stand firm as a solid, powerful truth.

This is the direction I face and the path I choose to take. When I come to the end of the road, I may find I was completely wrong; at least I will know that I found the answers for myself and did not base my entire life on hearsay.

Chapter 22
Winds of Change

In February 1997, as I began the final process of readying this book for publication, I noticed a definite change in activity around me.

Anomalous incidents have been occurring regularly at my home. Poltergeist activity has increased. Lights turn themselves off and on, unusual sounds echo through my house, and at times I feel blasts of bone-chilling cold. One evening I felt the physical sensation of a push to my shoulder from behind where I was sitting. There was nothing behind me but a wall.

On one occasion, I was listening to a CD on my stereo while making final changes to this book on my computer. After about five songs, the music stopped. I looked up to see that the CD compartment door on the stereo had popped open of its own accord. No one was near the stereo when this happened.

This type of activity has increased at my home. It is easy to dismiss an occasional strange occurrence, but these things have been happening daily. This time I have decided to stand my ground and refuse to let fear rule my emotions. When these things happen, I pray for the entity involved, and I pray for protection for those I love. The sensations of a presence remain with me for a while, but I am not paralyzed with fear. I become aggressively loving toward any non-physical entities I sense. This reaction seems to work.

I feel that I have experienced some activity that relates to the alien presence as well. One night I felt a strange sensation in my chest that frightened me. I felt as if I were about to have either a heart attack or an out-of-body experience. Because I could not differentiate between the two possibilities, I fought the feeling.

A few months earlier, I had been reading books about the out-of-body experience and silently wishing I could experience this for myself. It seemed to be another step in learning to accept myself as a spiritual being. I wanted to know if it was possible to separate from my physical body and have a controlled OBE.

Perhaps this was what was happening as I lay in my bed feeling as if I were preparing to separate from my body. It felt too much like dying, and I did not feel ready to take the risk. I know I have to lose my fear of death. I feel confident that I will continue on in spirit, but for now, I have too much left to do in this physical world.

I lay in bed, thinking of the possibilities of what was happening to me, when I began to see a stream of information scrolling above me toward the ceiling. It seemed to be a screen of symbols passing across my line of vision. The screen appeared to be about eighteen inches wide and passed from one wall to another in what appeared to be a beam of information. I do not remember any of the symbols I was shown, but I felt pumped full of information. As this was happening, my adrenaline was flowing and I was wide awake.

I do not remember falling asleep after that, but I awoke at 5:30 AM, feeling as if I had not slept at all. I had an underlying feeling that something else had happened, but I could not recall anything.

Several days later, I attended an abductee support-group meeting. During that meeting, I found that three other people recently had been shown information to read, but in different formats than I had experienced. None of us could recall any of the information we had been given.

I began to feel that something was happening and that a change was imminent. I was reflecting on this when I received a message statement in my mind. It said, "*You are going on-line.*" The impression I felt was not that we were going to be using a computer, but that we (abductees) are soon to be connected with each other. I don't know if this will occur through implants or consciousness.

I started getting impressions of earth changes coming soon. I tried to gather any understanding of what may be happening. I had a recurring thought that there would be an earthquake on the New Madrid fault soon, possibly this summer (1997). There was no other information, except a feeling that the quake would be more than a tremor. I don't know if it will be the Big One, but it will be big enough to cause alarm.

I watched the made-for-TV movie about an asteroid hitting the Earth and began to feel a vague uneasiness. Several months earlier, I had been outside watching an annual meteor shower and was spooked by a thought that came to mind. It was an image of a bright ball of light appearing in the sky and slamming to earth. I felt very vulnerable under
the night sky.

After the asteroid movie, I saw several different news programs exploring the possibilities of an asteroid hitting Earth and an explanation of the resulting devastation. I began to wonder if scientists knew something that they were not telling us. I had had several dreams of seeing a wall of fire coming over the horizon, rolling in my direction and destroying everything in its path. Was this our future? In one dream, I watched the wall of fire come toward me and quickly engulf me before I could react. I felt a flash of heat and knew instantly that I was dead. In the flames, I saw buffalo running, seemingly unhurt by the fire. I got an impression that the fire was cleansing the earth as the beginning of a renewal.

Another recent impression I received began with a feeling of my life shifting into high gear. It seemed that, suddenly, my spirit had accelerated, and I was living at a faster pace. It was a feeling of everything happening at once, and of having too little time to do everything I need to do.

While I was reflecting on this feeling, I received a very strong message statement in my mind. It said, "*The Ark is coming.*" This thought gave me goose bumps. I had talked with researchers and experiencers many times concerning the idea of a mother ship coming to pick up a percentage of Earth's population to take them to another place—possibly to assure a continuation of humanity in the event of a global catastrophe.

I had several dreams about this possible future event. I recall standing on the ground in the midst of mass confusion. Overhead, many huge spacecraft sat motionless in the sky. Meanwhile, I gathered people together to be taken up to the craft. In the dreams, I had been delegated the responsibility of making sure a specific group of people arrived on board. I hurriedly searched for faces I knew and felt an urgency to complete this task. At least one of the dreams included strong winds, storms, and an unusual color of sky.

Many other experiencers have reported dreams similar to mine. We have often discussed the meaning of these dreams and wondered if the event was something that would happen soon. When I received the statement of the "Ark" coming, it was the first time I felt strongly that these dreams could become fact. The only feeling I have about the time frame is a recurring impression of some type of global disaster happening in 1998.

I do not know exactly what type of disaster may occur, but I feel strongly that it will affect a lot of people and may cause great loss of life. This disturbs me and is part of the reason I feel I must come to some understanding concerning death and the loss of loved ones.

I have lost several good friends in the last couple of years, and with each occurrence, I found myself shutting down emotionally. I was unable to attend the funerals of several friends who died. I feel that I take on the emotions of everyone around me, and the sorrow of others combined with my own grief is too much to bear. It is the emotional outpouring that I have been unable to withstand.

I am coming to understand that death is only a transition and that those who die are still very close to us. I feel the veil that separates this life from the afterlife is becoming very thin. Many times I have felt the presence of those who have passed on, and I believe I have received communications from several friends on the other side.

I hope I can gather enough understanding of death and the transition from physical to spirit that will enable me to be more supportive during a time of loss. I feel strongly that death is the natural graduation to a greater existence, but I fail to find comfort in this belief when I am faced with the loss of someone I know.

Perhaps death is just another control issue that I have to learn to understand. I believe most of us who have had to face the abduction experience have problems with the loss of control in our lives. I know several abductees who exhibit overly controlling personalities in their "regular" lives as if to make up for the loss of control during abductions.

I am the opposite. I have had trouble throughout my life in giving others too much control. During the promiscuous phase of my life, I felt unable to say no, even when I knew I did not want to become involved with a particular person. I felt I could not resist and that something bad would happen if I said no. Since I have come to understand this about myself, I have been able to work on this aspect of my behavior. It is difficult because I have to reverse a lifetime of being unassertive. It is much easier to see the control issue problem in others' lives than to recognize the problem in myself.

March 27, 1997

The world has a strange way of providing synchronicities in our lives that reveal truth. This morning I turned on my television to hear the news of the day. The big news was the reported mass suicide of 39 individuals in California. These people believed their bodies were containers housing the soul. They reportedly believed a UFO was coming in the tail of the Hale-Bopp comet. The members committed suicide to
shed their bodies in order to meet this craft in a spirit form.

I was shocked as the information on the news continued to get stranger. I was also worried that the media would distort the truth in a manner that would have negative repercussions for people like me.

We have to come together and talk about these matters instead of placing blame on people of differing beliefs. Things are happening out there, and we cannot keep pretending that nothing is going on.

I do not know what these people believed in. I was approached by several members of this group three years ago. I had participated in a panel discussion at a UFO conference during the time I was having my fearful phase. I had voiced several fears during the panel discussion. After the talk, some women who sympathized with my fear problem approached me. They said I should come with them—that they could give me some of the answers I was looking for. At the time, my inner warning system sounded an alarm. These women were very nice, but very intense, and I always steer clear of anyone who claims to have all the answers. No one has all the answers. Each of us has been given a piece of this large puzzle, but no single soul has all the answers.

I excused myself from the company of these women as politely as I could. Later that weekend someone warned me that the "Bo and Peep" people were in the area and said I should not get involved with them. I remembered this experience as a brush with a fringe group. I have met many unusual people at UFO-related events, and I try to use my inner radar to protect myself from danger.

My greatest fear at this time is the coming reaction of the general public and the extent to which the media will say anyone who believes in UFOs belongs to a cult. That is very wrong. I hope the public will be intelligent enough to know the difference.

This incident seems to accentuate my opinion that people will continue to feel the Influence, and some will not have the strength of will to resist any unusual impulses. As long as we turn a blind eye to the possibilities of other intelligences interacting with our population, we become vulnerable to the influence of these entities. For years the media have treated the subject of UFOs as a joke. How many more will die before they realize it is not a laughing matter?

One other aspect of the effect of this event is apparent in the writing of this chapter. The impressions I related in the beginning of this chapter seem to represent a reflection of an Influence that also may have touched the 39. I was having recurring thoughts of death accompanied by an impression of going out of my body. Was I being given a choice at that time? My feelings of being not ready to die and an expression of a desire to live must have been my choice in the matter. Did these people feel the same Influence? The earlier message of "*You are going on-line*" and the mention that "*The Ark is coming*" combined with feelings of global disaster make me wonder what is happening to me and others.

I also was fascinated with the Hale-Bopp comet. I longed to see it. When I finally did see it, I was filled with emotion. I felt a connection to the event and was excited by the rare chance to see this comet that would not return for another 3,000 years. I was surprised by the many people I talked to who had no desire to see this celestial object. In early history, comets were always signs of some global consequence. Today it seems many people don't want to take the time to look up into the sky to view such an interesting object. We become so wrapped up in the trivialities of everyday life that we have no time to witness the wonders of this vast universe.

I don't know what to make of the current events and how the future will be played out. I realize I am ready to make a public stand to say what I believe is happening because the people have a right to know. I am ready to face any confrontation that may occur. This book is part of my purpose for being. I must say these things in the hope of sharing some understanding and lessening fear of the unknown. I hope I will not be a victim of "blaming the messenger for the message." I have done my best to explain my own experiences in as precise a way as possible. This book is my piece of the puzzle. It is time to combine our individual pieces of this global puzzle in order that we may find the answers together.

Epilogue

This story continues into the present. What I have shared with you is only the first phase of my dealings with this experience. My discovery has led me in many different directions. I continuously have to search my soul for answers to difficult questions.

What does it all mean? I have drawn no concrete conclusions. I have learned a few things along the way. The Visitors do not wear hats of black or white like good and bad guys should. They would probably wear gray. There are no clear-cut answers. I do not know what the consequences of my involvement will be. These strange beings appear to thrive on secrecy (as does our own government).

I have discovered that the aliens have very advanced technological abilities. They can make persons, places, and things appear and disappear as if by magic. At times they can control our thoughts and cause our bodies to respond in any way that suits their needs. Giving up control is probably the most difficult aspect of my experience.

My greatest questions lie in the helplessness I feel in the presence of these small, gray entities. Can these little humanoids force us to do things that we feel are morally wrong? I believe they can. Would they? That is an unknown. Should we expect an alien species to adhere to our sociological viewpoint?

I have had to participate in some distasteful and frightening examinations and experiments. At no time did I feel evil from the grays. I felt only their indifference to my emotional reactions. Determining the parameters of morality of a species that is so vastly different from our own is very difficult. They seem not to understand the depths of our emotions. They show strong curiosity about our emotional reactions to stimuli. They study those reactions intently.

Fear is one emotion that is easily accessible to the visitors. The abduction experience can generate a tremendous amount of fright. The sudden appearance of the grays is always shocking. And they have forced me to face my deepest personal terrors. My abductions have frightened me to a degree that I never thought possible. I am amazed at the level of fear that I have experienced. I have stood nose to nose with it and made its acquaintance. It is hard to explain how I could withstand it and be able to function normally afterward. The mind has tremendous coping mechanisms. I survived it and emerged a much stronger person.

One of the most significant lessons I have learned is the recognition of my inner strength. For most of my life, I absorbed fearful memories into my subconscious. We are easily controlled by the things that frighten us. The more we surrender to them, the more freedoms we lose. I have learned to battle fear with love.

During the most frightening and painful moments, I felt a presence, a "voice" urging me to keep on fighting. The voice was full of love and concern. I feel the voice is my connection to God, the Supreme Being, the Higher Power or whatever name you prefer to call Him. That is the voice I cling to when times are tough. It is my source of strength.

I have grown in so many ways—mostly in the knowledge of who I am as a human being on this planet. I have learned of the necessity to recognize my connection to all life. What I do to others, good or bad, I do to myself. We live a fragile existence on this place we call Earth. Few of us really appreciate what we have.

I think one difference between me and someone who has not had this experience is that I realize change is on the horizon. I watch people move about in their daily lives and routines. Most have lulled themselves into believing this everyday pattern of work and play is all that will ever be. I think disruption is inevitable. Many will not be able to withstand the changes ahead. Most people have a curiosity about other intelligent life in the universe. Very few want to meet that life personally.

The friendships I have made with the people I have met are among the most beneficial and enjoyable aspects of this experience. People who have experienced similar events in their lives have been of great help to me. These are people who have had amazing experiences—people full of life and strength and wonder, who fear publicity and prefer to remain anonymous but are searching for answers and understanding in their own ways. We are all very different. After one has interacted with other, vastly diverse intelligent life forms, the minute differences in the human species seem so trivial.

I have begun to see all life as a beautiful tapestry. We are all different shapes, sizes, and colors when viewed singly. We all have special qualities and gifts that are unique. Our diversity should be cherished. We are all individual threads in this tapestry of life. It is only when our individuality connects and is woven together that we are able to see the Big Picture that our wonderful and colorful diversity has created.

Along with emotional turmoil and unanswered questions, I feel that these experiences have given me a much-needed wake-up call. These intrusions have forced me to look inward into my soul and explore every part of who I am. How will we ever understand the Visitors if we do not understand ourselves?

I think it is important that we not take each abduction scenario at face value. There is much emotional manipulation, and the entities can create any situation with holographic imagery. I absorb, but do not believe, everything I see during an experience.

I am trying to understand changes I make in my life as a result of emotional reactions to my perceived experiences. Images seen during abductions may be genuine, or they may be illusions. My reactions to the images are real. The combined responses of each person involved in this enigma may be exerting subtle changes in the consciousness of mankind. These changes may be necessary for our survival. I am withholding judgment until the Big Picture comes into focus.

The Visitors have disrupted my life. They slip in and out of this world undetected. Their motives remain secret, and most of my questions remain unanswered. I never know when these beings will appear again. I have no protection against recurrences. They come and go with insolent ease and leave me reeling with the emotional aftermath. I wake up and go to work, pretending nothing has happened. I am one of many. I think it is about time we all quit pretending.

Because of these experiences, I have become more aware of what it means to be human. What wonderfully unique creatures we are! I believe the one thing that makes us so special is our ability to love. I think love is a power that is greatly underestimated. It is a power that I draw on daily. If something scares me or causes me pain, I fight back with love.

I do not love these strange creatures unconditionally. I do not welcome our "Space Brothers" with open arms. They will have to earn my love and respect. I fill myself with the love of family, friends, and humanity. Bad things may still happen, but that will never destroy my soul. Someday I hope all of these different creatures and cultures can coexist peaceably. I think it could happen. I am waiting for that day. Until that time comes, I will remain cautiously hopeful and joyfully human.

Appendix A
Telepathic Communications
Received by Jeanne Robinson

Many of these statements are incomprehensible to the author and editors; however, they are faithfully reproduced in the hope that they may be understandable to physicists or others. The indented portions of this section are quoted as nearly verbatim as possible, including some incorrect grammar and usage.

ECOLOGY

An ecological warning, apparently about the loss of the ozone layer and acid rain:

> 1. *In the cell distribution exist developing mutations adapting to the increased radiation of the biosphere. Lowered reproduction possibilities with the higher order mammals due to neutinate reduction. Deferred reaction to*

*colostrum failure. Carbon in lower atmosphere develop-
ing negative ingestion of the natural population of surface
dwellers. Blockage of the needed photosynthesis while
tainting precipitation to botanical life forms. Deoxidiza-
tion containment failure. High-level carcinogens absorbed
through epidermal layer.*

A communication referring to a rumor of a reported object that was being tracked by the Jet Propulsion Laboratory. The object was reported
to have made several course changes:

*2. The object that you speak of is of a nature not to be dis-
closed to you at this time. Be aware that this object is indeed on a trajectory that will rendezvous with your planet.
Continue observations and heed previous warnings. Remember that the foolish trivialities of war among members
of your own species will be greatly overshadowed by concerns of global preservation in the near future. Our observations are not to be considered threats. Our purpose
is to inform.*

A message I received while sitting on a creek bank. It seems to refer to
a pole shift:

*3. When all is once again covered by oceans, the sins of
your technologies will be purged and the world will begin
again. The land where you sit was once a sea of great
magnitude. The earth's upheaval altered the face of the
land, as it will again alter it in the future.*

*4. The situation on your planet is a volatile pit of danger-
ous possibilities. Do not forget how quickly life could
change and deteriorate. The combination of nuclear war-
heads and commercial reactors is a time bomb of radiation*

waiting for the inevitable moment of human error. All efforts should be made in the ending of any new construction of nuclear facilities.

Your planet is dying. Oil spills, radiation, and poisonous atmosphere all are taking their tolls. It is a pity, especially for your children. They will inherit the worst of what will come. There are not many options. We can evacuate some of you. We could take control of your entire population in order to keep the poison from infecting other worlds. You have used up your resources. Technology in the hands of fools. The ones in power have no conscience. They are blinded by greed and corruption.

This is why we have chosen certain individuals for migration. Most are not damaged by affluence. Some have gained riches in their lifetime. These will be carefully evaluated in the future. Some will go, others will not.

Those who are taken will be taught of the mistakes that have led to the ruination of life on your planet. They will be made aware so the mistakes will not be repeated by future generations.

5. Teleportation delays in converted ecosystems soon to be relegated for maximum efficiency. A comment on earthquakes and natural disasters to come in the Midwestern United States.

6. Epeirogenic upheavals in the eastern portions creating altered flow of the great river. This occurring from shifting fault line. Disruption of lifestyle, loss of life in greater urban area. Increase in tornadic activity. Warnings about the destruction of rain forests and damage to the earth's atmosphere.

Received October 14, 1991:

7. *Decimated botanical organisms eradicated by greedy industrialists and indigent tribal populations. Residual filum not hardy enough to replenish. Oxygenation of lower atmosphere depleted. Upheaval of natural life cycle. Thermal backlash in the ocean of life. 7.5 depletion code 12 in effect. Denigration forthcoming as conditions worsen. Reversion index narrowing daily. High-level carcinogens contributing to cell mutation in all species. Life-sustaining properties unbalanced as changes occur in abnormal systems. Analytical suppositions ineffective in the face of self-annihilation.*

THE ALIEN PURPOSE AND OTHER MISCELLANEOUS ADVICE
(A communication received on May 9, 1992):

8. *Parabiosis of selected equable genera is being utilized to establish mutually beneficent cohesive relationships. This allows our observers to integrate themselves into the sociological conditions of your planet. Melioration of the population of a predetermined area can be manipulated to optimum levels of behavior. The parity of synergetic species can develop an understanding that can adapt to the philosophy of interplanetary/interdimensional socialization. The zenith of this adaptability will be the basis of worldwide overt contact.*

9. *We study many of your people. The majority of these have not been able to accept us. They are crippled by fear-frightened creatures who are unable to see the experience in any positive way. Admittedly, the physical experiments are somewhat painful and traumatic. It is under these stressful conditions that we are able to test the strength and adaptability of our study group. Those who withstand the trauma and are able to face us with forgiveness, acceptance, and open curiosity are who we consider*

"chosen." These we consider as potential travelers—ones who could interact with our kind without fear, anger, hate, or prejudice.

10. Quiescence of the alternative support structure. Microcosm of regulated test subjects will be delegated to ininsic life studies. Calibration of the transceiver receptors will heighten awareness of the existence of other subjects and instinctive holistic conversion.

11. Cultivation of the 243 million test subjects is most illuminating in the desired educational planetary study.

An explanation of cattle mutilations and tissue sampling:

12. It is important that your people realize the necessity of our actions concerning selected animal species. These occurrences seem brutal by your standards and are greatly misunderstood. We do not kill for sport. We mourn any loss of life. All life is precious.

Substances taken are used for the preservation of many lives. Recombined genetics and biosynthetic generation of isolated cell structure are matters of conservation of higher life forms. Tissue is removed by photolytic beams, which transude the selected area of cellular composition.

Concerning secrecy and sociological impact:

13. In the times ahead, there will be upheavals of society. There will be a time when previous realities will be shattered by the awareness of what is truth. Before that time, there will be major disagreements between those who are becoming involved in new awareness and those frantically trying to avoid change. It will be a troubling time. Cer-

tain religious groups will be avid opponents to what we are attempting to share with you.

There will also be conflicts with those who wish to keep the truth hidden in the area of UFO research. Be strong in your beliefs, and do not be intimidated. It will not be an easy time, but the truth will make itself known.

Who are the "Pleiadians"?

14. *It is a sect within an ancient, highly advanced culture. There were both good and evil members of this group. At one time, highly respected but disrupting factions created chaotic situations beyond repair.*

15. *Early man was placed upon Earth in an experimental evaluation of the living conditions of your planet. Visitors to your planet interbred with these creatures on several occasions. While their motives were less than honorable, it did begin the process of evolution of your species. Our intervention in your life on a physical level is for further evolution of your species and ours. Your children have been placed on another world, in much the same way your early ancestors were placed upon Earth.*

16. *We have been willing to offer you an exchange of information that would increase understanding of our vastly different cultures. When your species learns to accept the reality of our existence, much can be gained from this knowledge. Denial of other intelligent life forms is the natural response of self-preservation within the egocentric society. There comes a time when your species must adapt. As a child comes of age to face the harsh truths of adulthood, so must your species mature and accept its place in the universal family. We can help you in your transition. You are not alone. Relinquish your isolation*

and gain strength with your knowledge.

This message seemed like a group of fragmented thoughts:

17. *There is essential meaning behind the words we give to you. We share elements of truth with the need for a fundamental reality. You cannot grasp the idea of logical science. Biomorphic notation in selected spheres. Emotional extraction is for educational indoctrination.*

Hints of a one-world government (Received February 24, 1991):

18. *The development of awareness of universal life increases within the mainstream of your population. The growing involvement of your people, in passing relevant information to the unknowing, is being observed by our council of advisors.*
    The danger of armed conflict has reached a level of moderate stabilization. We continue surveillance in this region of your planet in order to remain alert to any global dangers that may exist.
    There is a need for the unification of the nations of your world. A world policy must be formed in order to control the less civilized members of humanity. It is necessary to forget past grievances and unite as a species. This can be done without the loss of territorial boundaries of the individual ethnic consensus. This global network would be overseen by the heads of nations in a council of world leaders. Technology, information, and other resources could be shared in a betterment of nations. For example, the Union of Soviet Socialist Republics has knowledge and strength that could be exchanged for agricultural technology. The walls of distrust must be evaluated and agreements drawn up in order to facilitate

unification.

The world is in preparation for our involvement. We are now contacting individuals in virtually every nation on your planet. The heads of state are being informed of this need to unify. This is a recent development drawn from mutual involvement of scientific socialization. This drive to global understanding and preparedness is currently being termed "the New World Order." It is a positive effort to make amends for the irrational reaction of contact between our two species. The power of the original perpetrators of the code of silence now lessens. The violence of the agency of deceit will be overcome. Your world is in preparation for new awareness.

You are involved in this change facing your planet. All those currently working in the field of extraterrestrial research are necessary elements in the formation of educational developments within the psyche of your population. You will assist in making the change less frightening. Be aware that the changes you have observed during the last year are not chance happenings. Your involvement has been orchestrated in a compilation of experiential data.

Those involved in electronic media are desensitizing the population from their fear of contact with other intelligent species. The majority of your people are now mentally capable of accepting this reality. Our mutual acceptance will grow to a time when open contact will be possible.

You must now prepare and grow in order to participate in this change. Your ability as biological transceiver will be needed in maintaining contact and the exchange of data. This will increase understanding of our purpose in a less intimidating means of contact.

Regarding events in the Soviet Union (Received August 24, 1991):

19. *The human consciousness is evolving to unified*

awareness. The bonds of oppression are no longer strong enough to control the masses. The percentage of population which has been given the ability to precipitate change has been activated. The sociological implications are endless.

Primitive tyranny will no longer be tolerated. You are not yet aware of the imperceptible pressure being exerted on the human consciousness, but you are beginning to see the results. Is it not yet obvious to you? The threat of nuclear annihilation was once so great the nervous finger was trembling on the trigger of Armageddon. Self-destruction was imminent. The decision to intervene was the alternative to massive destruction. Your leaders are aware of the intervention. However, the controlling powers were not willing to concede that they could no longer rule the multitudes with an iron thumb of fear and violence. Their own fear was too great. The last attempt at grasping to the old ways was futile.

This is only the beginning. Your hemisphere will soon experience a radical upheaval of its own. The once warring factions will learn to depend upon each other for survival. While the fools still vie for supremacy, an undercurrent of applied humanity will develop and prepare for contact with their genetic benefactors, who eagerly await the convergence.

Concerning Saddam Hussain:

20. *Indications of heightened tensions between disagreeable nations are the result of nuclear potential of primitive culture controlled by sociopathic leader. Substantial evidence of biological weaponry, as well as chemical development. Plutonium cache in center of civilian population. Underground network of terrorist activity. Essential ingredients stored in holy shrines.*

21. *Concerning the situation of the planet, we have made several observations. Your officials are hiding the evidence of increasing occurrences within your atmosphere. Several incidents have been brushed over to silence the inquiries.*

It is necessary to deepen a search to reveal the hidden truths. There is an increasing effort to control governmental officials at a lower level of rank. Distrust is of a greater force. Silence will not be maintained. Frequency of occurrences will soon be of a magnitude that no one will be able to hide all information available. Prepare for an overwhelming degree of appearances and physical manifestations in your area. The location in which you live is chosen for multilateral displays. All phases of contact will be increased. Prepare for this as your world awakens from hibernation of winter.

This message was given specifically to be presented to the public (Received in April 1991):

22. *We are communicating this information through the biological transceiver in order to share data with your population.*

We have been with you for many years. It has been necessary to conceal our studies of your planet. Your people fear what they do not understand. This fear creates a hazard for us.

Your planet contains essential properties for the survival of our species. We have a form of hypoplasia that restricts the natural reproductive capabilities. We are able to bypass these restrictions by taking active genetic cultures and developing fertile zygotes by various means including biosynthesis. Evaluation in parasynapsis denotes the vascular tissue is syncronious in both species.

Photosynthetic properties are induced by alteration of molecules and chromosome splicing.

We have researched your physiology to understand the elements that are parallel to our own. We mean you no harm, but we must save ourselves from extinction. You would do the same if situations were reversed.

We are also formulating the effects of emotional stimuli on the chemical responses within brain cells—particularly, adrenaline reactions as a protection within the biochemical structure.

When acceptance of the reality of our kind is tolerated within your population, a more open relationship can begin. An exchange of information and cultures can be beneficial.

We are not gods, and we are not devils. We are only an alternate life form. We are alike, and yet we are different. We can coexist in the universe and thrive on mutual understanding. We speak to you in this manner because we are afraid of your fear of us. This fear creates volatile situations that must be avoided. We will continue covert contact for now. Soon we will be able to establish a more active and cohesive relationship—an equal partnership within the alliance of intelligent life forms.

23. The levels of authority within the exploration quadrant of your planet are varied. Within your personal contact group are several species, each of which must account for their actions. The high command council presides over the research element. This group observes actions and assures adherence to strict regulatory commitments.

The council advisor in your own consanguineous development has been Zanopria the Elder (praying mantis type). Adherence to authority during metagenetic procedures and the communicative process is relayed through the council advisor.

There are other species within the command council,

and delegates vary from case to case. Each species has its own motivational needs of contact with your planet. Any deviation from mandated policy is noted and conciliation procedures are used to rectify the problem when possible.

Those violating protectionism are expunged from research.

An explanation of crop formations:

24. *Controlled gravitational thrust in selected botanical generations viably resulting in reverse stasis of natural metabolism. Formations in altered flow. Rapid reduction of molecular density in fluid containment levels. Fluctuations in electromagnetic impulses of cellular tissue. Purpose being continued awareness of the forces of change in planet's evolutionary process. Renewal of forgotten symbolic cultural demagogue [demigod?] in primitive society.*

25. *Control of the masses is necessary to ensure the expedient recovery and revitalization of your planet.*

BIOLOGY:

26. *Tabulation of impulse registering in intercellular neuronic activity in order of occurrence. Microbiotic energy emissions within the brain cells is the essence of the integration of the physical body and the energy that is the soul.*

27. *Mutation of tissue bombarded by radiation alters cell division to erase DNA/RNA memory wholly or in part to begin reproduction of irregular molecular bonding in retrograde.*

28. *The geometric element of the visual spectrum can be manipulated to precise equations creating a tranquilizing effect. The stimulation of brain waves by the optic nerve initiates chemical responses in the endocrine glands. The thought process can be more thoroughly analyzed by transmission of electronic imaging of the neuron functions. A cathode tube connected into the brain tissue by micro-probes into the area of cerebrum fold. Sense stimulation induced by activation of intercellular electroshock to simu-late brain-wave impulse.*

29. *Fibroplasia generated with corticosterone substitute, increase of collagen regrowth.*

Concerning animal/cattle mutilations:

30. *Crystalline structural composition within collected tis-sue altered to eliminate decay. Mineral formation in bio-logical fluid samples extracted. Protein generated to DNA reconstruction of formulated tissue. Ribonucleic acid growth with controlled systems removed.*
Increase in tissue-sample collection of bovine species. Similarities in genetic makeup of human tissue. Samples extracted for varied uses. Pollutants registered in areas selected for study. Absorption of harmful substances re-vealed in tissue of mucous membranes. DNA uses also to be increased in collected data. The cellular tissue and or-gans extracted by concentrated beam of photon energy. Fluids extracted and circulatory system infused with hy-drostatic substitute.

31. *Intricate design of molecular substructures of DNA composition relays inherited deficiencies as well as posi-tive traits and physical type. Genetic splicing of individual chromosomes within DNA matrix can be used to eliminate*

unfavorable traits and physical flaws which make a stronger race. The improved product can then pass on advanced biological systems to future generations, which effectively evolves the species. Genetic alteration increases intellectual capacity of a larger percentage of the brain than the amount currently in use. By choosing the chromosomes that control the areas of specific interest, it is possible to achieve varied results. While the life span could be lengthened ten-fold, it is not advised—that is, until your kind can adequately provide for the needs of the population already in existence.

32. Intellectual capacity of the higher order mammals can be increased by genetic restructuring of DNA code. Fractional alterations imprinted with electromagnetic impulses initiate cellular responses. Accelerated learning capacity begins by first opening the paths of thought and stimulation in repeated signals to retrain brain cells to respond accordingly.

33. Multiplicity of bioplasmic cell structure degenerates during aging process. Code memory dilutes during regeneration, breaking down DNA.

34. Tabulation of impulse registering in intercellular neuronic activity in order of occurrence. Microbiotic energy emissions within the brain cells are the essence of the integration of the physical body and the energy that is the soul.

PHYSICS

35. Reconstructive filaments within the fractal spectrum will illumine positive density fluctuations of the composite field of optical sensors. Prismatic deviation of light emis-

sions controls the amount of detectable influence of particles of matter in the volume of chemical components of radiation and the physical elements of atmospheric decay.

36. *Controlled emissions of microwave into the limitless vacuum of consistent gravitational inertia will stabilize and reflect on particles of matter reverberating with equal force the kinetic radiation of emitted energy to the wave front.*

37. *Cyclotronic generation of adjusted flux in cohesion, with elemental fusion of inherent DNA. In addition, photon diffusion pertaining to the coefficient of the altered properties is essential for quantum movement in relation to time and space continuum.*

38. *Trillium* [tritium?] *sulfate combines in strictured pressurization filters energy particles to a point of active return necessary for condensation of quanta in formatting restructuring of molecular protoplasm when the adjustments are traced to a proper source.*

39. *Bilateral confined atrium* [Yttrium?] *heated to a level of reformed matter in which the changes are used in a formula that is applied to the infusion of electrons and is passed in a conduit of neutral* [neutronic?] *ionization.*

40. *Fluctuations of electrostatic pulse indicates conditions of dark matter and other nonvisible particles in the density of interstellar distances. False echoes.*

41. *In the event of elemental fusion, conventional dilinear applications are no longer relevant. Diametric systems profile must be developed to strengthen coherent properties in the movement of molecular content. Sublevel analyses prove fractional control of neutron core. Future*

applications are arranged in maximum frequency of atomic reverberation within the helix at levels of micronetic vibration. The genetic influence within the confines of cell tissue of symbiosis and interconnection within cytoplasmic core regulate deviant DNA/RNA mutation from radical isotopes of + 679.3572 intensification.

42. *Fractional deviation from the structural containment value of the subatomic radiation field will neutralize ionized particles in condensed matter. Heightened phontonic absorption into layered veils or filters will alter visual spectrum to project only minimal visual stimulation of the optic nerve. This program can be implemented to disguise or formulate false images depending upon the needs of the moment. Holographic images can be formatted from the substance of enhanced matter into the spectrographic envelope of artificial fabrication into the light generation transmitter. False images placed in controlling wave generation used for instruction, indoctrination, or communication of select subjects.*

43. *Fragments of dispersed matter developing into ionized field of intense gravitation. Absorbing all radiation within circle of influence. Field density capable of effecting magnetic impulses.*

44. *Sequential Doppler waves accessing random reciprocal contacts vibrate continuous frequency of tone. Fluctuating sequence indicates a disruption of dark matter in the vacuum of interstellar distances.*

45. *Conventional physics influenced by intervention in continued contact of select life forms. Experimental relationships developed in accord with high command. Intellectual evaluation of desired effect registered within the confined data. Heightened brain-wave stimulation in-*

creases with each transmission, expanding conceptual reasoning.

46. *Teleportation delays in converted ecosystems soon to be relegated for maximum efficiency.*

47. *Dilinear convergence of mass and energy forming congruent plasma core. Highly soluble atmospheric reaction to converse colloid in systematic ionization of oxygenated sphere. Compressed atoms of hydrogen with cerium influx. Beryllium influence of the structural compound forcing antimatter cell of newly formed negatron into intradimensional tunneling effect. Many realities coexisting in parallax.*

48. *Hydrolytic power base of concurrent wave impulse. Fortric insulation of composed liquefaction of inert gaseous system. Force 12 linear cross-representation within formula stabilizer is productive stimulator of atomic reverberation in vacuum. Funnel effect accentuated by vacuum control of antimatter coil. Absorption of light emission as well as all radio energy sources within confined system. Compressed radiation absorbed into collector base to magnify power intensity of fiber accentuator. Energize coil into projected subspace target quadrant releasing fission control block. Release of vacuum control forces burst of radiated energy towards pressurized attenuator to be directed as a beam of photon radiation and/or gravitational wave.*

SPIRITUALITY

49. *There are other dimensions or life levels. We are able to enter these if there is a need. There is an area of movability that is a type of corridor to these life levels and to*

traverse time and space. We are from one of the other lev-els. It is different from yours in many ways.

There are levels nearly identical to your own. Others are more primitive, and there are highly advanced levels, also. Time is a river of experience constantly in motion. Your past is a dimension, like an echo that reverberates into the present and future and back again. What was, is, and will be has already occurred. It is the riddle of time fluctuation.

50. *There are no specific dimensions for the highly ad-vanced. Life levels are for the advancement of souls. The school of experience. The perfected soul needs no physical form. When you become attuned to the spirit within you, you touch the energy of all life. The life force is within you and all around you. When you know yourself well enough, you can blend your spirit with those of others. You can be one with all life. You did this as a child, pretending to be certain animals. You felt the energy of the creature. You tapped into the gracefulness and stealth of a cat, the joy and strength of a running horse. It was play for you, but the imagination and innocence of a child is a powerful force, often lost as the child matures. Native Americans knew these secrets, as did some primitive cultures. It was a form of religion. You can reach this oneness of life, and it will help you to appreciate all life as it exists in the Uni-verse.*

51. *Time is fluent-free-flowing existence of what was, what is, and what will be. All that has been leaves molecu-lar residue, which is an imprint of existence. Hence, the apparitions, seen by some, are molecular energy of lives past. Your existence in the present is an illusion of sub-stance. The energy of your being is capable of transforma-tion.*

Death is molecular transformation of matter. You are

energy, capable of reformation. Death is not the only way. It is difficult for you to grasp this information. The soul understands what the mind cannot. You are capable of transmigration to a new existence. The alteration of molecules is widely used in our culture. The power of the psyche is an untapped resource, which is available to you.

52. The physical substance of man entwined with the spiritual essence is governed by molecular bonding of cohesive energy. All of the physiological functions and properties are ruled by the cognizance of spiritual awareness.

The life energy of all living substances is infinitely connected as one massive, functioning unit. The energy confines itself in diverse composites of physical tissue, which creates experiential feedback to the creative source. The physical form dictates the level of controlled response, ranging from instinctual behavior to conscious thought.

The creative life force controls the physical world around it. After leaving the physical body, the spirit returns to the creative force from which it originated. On returning, it absorbs all data contained in the mass of life energy. In essence, your inner conscience contains all the data from all life preceding it.

53. There will be a time when all must come to terms with the lives they have lived. Those who have continually followed the path of evil, life after life, will be isolated with others of their ilk—isolated from the joy of goodness and light. Their evil will not be able to touch the perfected ones. They will be ignored, non-entities unable to arouse any reactions to their evilness.

It is a state of limbo, eternal isolation. It will be hell for those who have spent their lives thriving on the pain and fear and misery they caused to others. There they will learn to regret their choice of existence. Eternal, unchangeable regret.

The advanced souls will rejoice in communion with the Creator. A spiritual unity of love and peace and sharing. Blended spirits, one with God.

Many changes will soon occur. There is a solidarity in the spiritual nature of man. Individuals will reach new confirmations in their beliefs. The many tributaries of the Universal God will be increased. While there are vast differences in understanding, all will be aware of the coming dimensional shift. It will be a turbulent time.

The followers of good and evil will become more distinct. The humans of higher understanding will be altered to transverse consciousness. The lower, evil-natured beings will be left behind. This filtration will be complete near the time of the millennium. Many universal travelers are aware of this evolutional [evolutionary?] birthing process and are observing with great interest. It is a rare opportunity to observe the transformation of a polymorphic species.

54. The significance of your existence should not be randomly trivialized. You are still a child whose eyes are not yet opened to the changes and growth of your consciousness. The physical components of your substance is merely a cocoon housing the energy within. You will emerge a new being. Expanded awareness of your connection to the all-powerful creative force that connects the universe is at your disposal. You are a polymorph—a phoenix that will rise from the ashes. Do not fear what lies ahead, for you will emerge triumphant.

Appendix B
Transcript: Feeding the Babies

When I first began this book project, I received much advice. Some suggested I put all my hypnosis transcripts in the book. Others thought transcripts were dull reading.

I decided to write about the experiences that came partly from hypnosis and partly from conscious recall. For the transcript fans, I decided to include a sample of one hypnosis session. This will help the reader understand the technique and style of a hypnosis session.

What follows is only a partial transcript of one of my 15 sessions. It begins after I recalled a typical physical examination on a craft. "B. J." is an abbreviation of the pseudonym "Bill Johnson," which I used throughout the book to refer to my hypnotherapist.

B. J.: Okay, take a deep breath...looking at yourself, and you're ten years old.... You can step out and watch from the side.

J. R.: There's one at the door.... There's...another one coming in.

B. J.: So, you're taking a good look at the second one that comes in... What do you notice?

J. R.: He's got kind of a long...like cape or something. It's got a collar, and it's got this thing that pulls it right here, and lines come out.... I'm sitting up on the table.

B. J.: Okay.... So the second one came in the room with a cape?

J. R.: Uh-huh. It was kind of flowing back behind him.

B. J.: What about him? Or her?

J. R.: It's a him.

B. J.: How do you know?

J. R.: 'Cause I know him...

B. J.: When did you know him? From before?

J. R.: Uh-huh. He's the one I call "Grandpa."

B. J.: Didn't exactly look like Grandpa, did it?

J. R.: (Laughs) Uh-uh!

B. J.: So why did you call him "Grandpa"?

J. R.: He felt old like my Grandpa.... I don't know why I called him that.... Huh.

B. J.: Okay. Well, does it feel good to recognize him? You seem to kind of, uh, welcome him.

J. R.: Yeah...I don't know.... I just am not afraid of him.

B. J.: If they all look alike, I wonder how you recognized him?

J. R.: Um, he felt different.

B. J.: What do you mean? Physically?

J. R.: Uh-uh. Oh, just...I felt...he just...has a feeling about him...that I felt when he walked in.

B. J.: Okay. So, he comes breezing into the room, and...what happens?

J. R.: He says...it's good to see me.

B. J.: Do you feel the same way?

J. R.: No-o-o-o.

B. J.: You're not so sure! So, what else does he tell you?

J. R.: He asks me how I am.... I don't know.... I don't like this! He asks me if I want to go into the other room.... "Yes...." I do.... Um! I don't like this room.... Oh!..it's a room with big windows.

B. J.: Big windows? Have you seen that before?

J. R.: No.

B. J.: So you've just walked in and you notice all these big windows.

J. R.: Ohhhhh...there's...ohhhhh...ohhh! (Amazed by something.)

B. J.: Don't forget to tell me.

J. R.: (Gasps, taken aback by something.) I'm...way, way up! *Way* up.

B. J.: You kind of lost your stomach there for a minute, didn't you?!

J. R.: (Breathes sharply.) Ummm...Mama isn't gonna like this!

B. J.: I'm sure she wouldn't. So, you went over to the window, I guess, and looked out.

J. R.: It's pretty!

B. J.: What do you see?

J. R.: The planet. I guess it's the earth!

B. J.: What does it look like?

J. R.: Part of it's blue and brown and white and dark...on part of it.... I...must be dreaming!

B. J.: Is your stomach okay now?

J. R.: Yeah, I guess so.

B. J.: I thought you'd lost it there for a minute! So, what does he tell you...about what you've seen?

J. R.: He says, "This is how your earth looks."

B. J.: ...and you said, "Thanks, but I want to go home?"

J. R.: Uh, no...no.

B. J.: C'mon, tell me what you said.

J. R.: "How high up are we?"

B. J.: And, he said...?

J. R.: Oh...uhh...

B. J.: Did he answer you?

J. R.: Uh...yeah...but...it...he...it's too much.... We're too high up! It's ...something like a thousand...miles?

B. J.: Okay, how big did the earth look as you looked at it? Was it the size of a baseball, basketball, a house? How big does it look out there?

J. R.: It's...it's kind of big, but...

B. J.: Reach out your hand and try to touch each side of the image. You know what I mean? I mean, if it was too big, your arms would be stretched way out. If it was tiny, your thumb could cover it. See if you can reach out your hands and touch each side of the image you see...about there?

J. R.: Yeah.

B. J.: Roughly about a foot and a half....Your hands are about a foot and a half apart, okay. It's possible to correlate that with a thousand miles out. That's why I asked. Okay, go ahead now.... What seems to happen?

J. R.: Um...I asked him if he had a name.... He said, yep...it's...it's..."Queet-zow."

B. J.: "Queetzal...Queetzal...." Is this the first time you heard it?

J. R.: Yeah. Huh...uh, he says I'm special, and I should remember that...that I'm a part of something really special, and that's why they come to see me.

B. J.: It didn't really influence your life though, did it? Him saying that?

J. R.: No. Not...no, maybe just a feeling sometimes, but not much.... He wants to know if I'd like to help do something.... It's a special job...uh...they need me to do it.

B. J.: So do you...are you going to leave this room?

J. R.: Yeah.

B. J.: Well, before you do, I want you to take another look around, and see if you notice anything...other than the windows...and what shape the room is, and how it's lit...these kinds of things.

J. R.: It's, uh...ummm...not very bright and there's like...it's almost like a hallway. It's got...it looks like...chairs or a bench along the wall. It's round...looks like squishy chairs....There's...where the chairs are, there seems to be like a glass...dark, dark glass, round part...It's not very bright 'cause the brightness comes from looking out...

B. J.: Can you see your shadow from the Earth? You know what I mean?

J. R.: Uh-uh.

B. J.: The Earth is bright, and the room is dark....Do you notice that your jammies are lit up by the light?

J. R.: Yeah, there's a little—like a reflection on me and him.

B. J.: Well...take us to where he goes...and you go together.

J. R.: Okay. We go in this little...door...and it shuts.... It's like a...it must be an elevator or something.... We're moving.

B. J.: See any dials, buttons, or lights?

J. R.: No. There was a light the size of a.... It was like he waved his hand over me...and we're stopping.... It's bright...um...

B. J.: What's bright?

J. R.: The room. There's...ha!...there's these little things...little... sheesh! They're...like beds, I guess. They're like plastic and they... come out.... Then there's...babies!

B. J.: How many?

J. R.: (Counts to herself.) About eight...shoo.... What are they doing here? ...I ask him if they're his.... He said, "They belong to all of us."

B. J.: What did you think that meant when you heard it?

J. R.: Ohh...shoo, I don't know! He asked me if I want to feed them.... "I don't care...sure."

B. J.: So do they get out the milk bottles?

J. R.: No.

B. J.: Why not?

J. R.: There's some guys over here, doing something. They've got...a bowl... (gestures) oh, like that.... There's some stuff in it! Oo-oo-oh ...it stinks!

B. J.: What does it smell like...now that you're smelling it again...right now?

J. R.: It's real...kind of has an onion or garlic smell. It's got...(sighs). It's like beans, but it's not. It's real...strong.

B. J.: Does it look smooth and clear like Jello? Or...lumpy like apple-sauce?

J. R.: It's like apple butter...stinky apple butter.... "You guys eat this?" Phew!... "What do I...how do I...got a spoon? How do they...how?" He wants me to put my hands in it.

B. J.: What do you say?

J. R.: That's yucchh!

B. J.: Why does he want you to put your hands in it? Is that some way of washing your hands?

J. R.: He says that's the way...I will have to feed them. He takes me over to this wall. There's a hole in it....He says, "Stick your hands in there."

B. J.: Do you do that? I sure wouldn't! At ten years old? You're going to stick your hands in these two holes?

J. R.: It's one hole...."What is it? Is it going to hurt?" (Pauses.) He says it's just to clean them...like disinfectant.

B. J.: You feel like a blast of air or what?

J. R.: I stuck them in, and there was like...kinda almost wet-like steam stuff.

B. J.: Well, was it hot or cold?

J. R.: It was kind of cool.

B. J.: How long did that last?

J. R.: Not long...just, "SSSHHH!"

B. J.: Did you see anything...that went along with that?

J. R.: Yeah, like steam.

B. J.: Okay. And are your hands wet now?

J. R.: Yeah, they're both damp. "...Okay...." We're going to this first one.... "It's not very big."

B. J.: The baby's not?

J. R.: Uh-uh.

B. J.: What does it look like?

J. R.: Huh...it's like...one of them.

B. J.: Exactly?

J. R.: (Sighs.) I think so. I don't know....It's...let me look! ...It doesn't have any hair. Its eyes are big.... (Sighs.)

B. J.: Nice, round, little baby face?

J. R.: No, it looks mostly eyes.

B. J.: Did you...go on, go on.... What's the matter? ...What were you thinking?

J. R.: I just thought I saw something.

B. J.: Okay, back up for a moment...and in a second, you'll see it again, and then this time you'll be able to freeze-frame it.... Time will stop, and you can take a good look. One, two, now...

J. R.: Oh no! ...I don't see anything. There was something there.... It wasn't right.

B. J.: Where was this?

J. R. I don't know. I just... (Sighs.)

B. J.: What feeling did you get?

J. R.: Scared!

B. J.: So something scary flashed. Was it right in front of your face? Or was it down at your feet? Or in the crib?

J. R.: I thought it was in the crib...but I don't...I don't know where it came from.

B. J.: Are these little babies wearing anything?

J. R.: (Sighs.) Uh-uh...there's...

B. J.: They're naked?

J. R.: Yeah.

B. J.: What does the rest of their body look like?

J. R.: Skinny. Looks like a skinny bird...like a baby bird.... It's almost like you can see it inside.... It doesn't have much of a chest...long, skinny arms.... The head's kind of big.... It's looking at me.

B. J.: Does looking at the baby scare you? Does it looking at you scare you?

J. R.: No, it doesn't.... It's waiting.

B. J.: Ah, for the food! Do they cry at all?

J. R.: I don't hear anything from this one.... I'm supposed to put my hands in this stuff! How do they eat? (Laughs in amazement.) I'm supposed to take some...and rub it on...

B. J.: Yeah? Like on their face...and then they lick it off?

J. R.: Huh, weird.... Okay, I got to take it, and I rub it on their arms, their chest, tummy.... Okay! The back.... I'm supposed to rub it in... 'til it disappears.... I just rub it around.... Their little arms are so skinny!

B. J.: So, is it kind of like putting suntan lotion on?

J. R.: Uh-huh. It's like rubbing like lotion, but it stinks!

B. J.: Was it lumpy at all?

J. R.: Uh-uh...real smooth.... He likes it.

B. J.: How can you tell?

J. R.: (Speaks with a childlike voice.) I don't know. He just does.

B. J.: You mean he smiles at you?

J. R.: No.... He looks at me.... It's.... "It satisfies two hungers.... It feeds him...nutrients and...it eases...the hunger for touching."

B. J.: That's interesting. Now, you could tell that the baby likes this?

...How can you tell? What changes do you notice that makes you think that he likes it? I mean, if I rubbed it on a chair, I wouldn't know that the chair liked it! So how do you know that this little baby likes it?

J. R.: Just the same way.... I know what these...they're...thinking, but they don't say it.

B. J.: You get a feeling about it?

J. R.: Uh-huh.

B. J.: You like doing this now?

J. R.: Yeah...if it didn't smell so bad!

B. J.: Do you just get to do this one little baby?

J. R.: No.

B. J.: You mean, you do the whole bowl?

J. R.: No. Why don't they just sit them in the bowl?

B. J.: Is that what you asked him? What does he say?

J. R.: They would...suffocate...drown/suffocate. So, it wouldn't work ...Uh, huh...Uh-huh!

B. J.: You mean, if they sit in it, they might drown?

J. R.: Something like that..."Don't feed too much." ...There was another one. It wasn't like him. It was different....It's got eyes different... and...almost hair...fuzz...and it's bigger.... It's a girl.... (Sighs.) This one, um...doesn't eat the same way.... It sorta does.... It needs.... It drinks.... It had.... They have something...you know, squishy thing.... I can give her it...I guess like a bottle, almost. It's like a bag.

B. J.: Same smelly stuff in it?

J. R.: I don't think so. It's...it looks kind of clear.... I just...it reminds me...it's like those things you decorate cakes with. And it takes a little bit of it.

B. J.: Uh-huh. Do you see lips and a tongue and that kind of stuff?

J. R.: Kind of little lips.... I don't see a tongue.... I still got...put some of the stuff on her, too.

B. J.: Where did you put it on her?

J. R.: Same place.

B. J.: On her back? On her shoulder and chest and her tummy?

J. R.: Uh-huh.

B. J.: Does this baby make any sound?

J. R.: Yeah...it's real squeaky sound when it eats...when it was drinking.

B. J.: Okay....Did they communicate anything more about this whole process to you?

J. R.: Two of them...like them...are real special babies.... It's...hard for them to make babies...so, when it happens, they get special, special care.... They're just special...rare babies...that they don't...it's hard for them to make them.... They said...that they need our help with that...to make more babies.... There's not enough of them to survive.... They can't...reproduce...quick enough.

B. J.: I bet that was hard to understand at age ten.... What did you think they were talking about?

J. R.: (Sighs.) They...just need babies! Babies...that's something that they're doing.

B. J.: At that point in time, did you understand where babies came from?

J. R.: No.

B. J.: Did this confuse you a bit?

J. R.: Maybe.... I just didn't think about it much.

B. J.: Look around the room and see what else you notice...and tell me what happens.

J. R.: They turn this light on.... It's a light above them.... It's real bright...brighter than it already is! "You gotta bake them now?" "They need the light. It helps them digest." ...I want to stick my hands in that thing.

B. J.: Why? Oh...you mean that thing that cleans your hands?

J. R.: Uh-huh. It's sticky and stinky!

B. J.: Did you ever get a feeling—I know at age ten it may be hard to remember—but, a feeling of why they were showing you all this?

J. R.: Huh...they just...want me to learn about it. This will be my job someday.... Wow...I could think of other things I'd rather do!

B. J.: Yeah, I could, too! What happens now? Is this the end of your tour?

J. R.: Yeah.

Appendix C
Inspiration

I wrote the following poems and lyrics to express the emotions directly related to my experiences. These media of expression have helped me a great deal. I consider my poetry a positive byproduct of the abduction phenomenon.

I had been shy and fearful of my ability to sing since being hurt by a statement a music teacher made about my singing voice when I was just a preteen. Since the teacher was the "expert" in my young eyes, I believed I could not sing. I never sang in front of people after that.

In 1994-95, I began writing lyrics to possible songs. In 1996, I felt the desire to express myself musically. I felt I needed to be able to sing to fully express some of the material I had written. I took a big step in believing in myself. When my place of employment began to have a "karaoke night," I took a chance. I sang a song before many people. I received good feedback and was uplifted by a feeling of having overcome a personal emotional obstacle.

While I accept the fact I am obviously a writer, not a singer, I encourage others to believe in themselves instead of the opinions of others. The joy of singing should not be suppressed. Music has a significant positive effect on the soul, and it is a great feeling to be able to express oneself with a song.

I would like to share the following poems in order to show that there can be a positive, creative effect from even the most bizarre of experiences:

Infiltration

They are calling me again.
Such blinding fear chills my soul
As I flip the latch and step outside.
This heart pounds frantically in my chest.
I feel my fragile humanity collapse.
Looking up, it's there above me.
Quarter moon reflects upon the silver metal.
Heaven's galleon glows above the treetops.
I want to run!
I want to hide!
Standing motionless, I wait
As the curtain of searing blue energy
Envelopes my primitive innocence
And genetic history.
Unwilling participant of interstellar research,
Immersed in a multitude of wonders,
Until, once again, released
Tired and used in the early hours
Of a new emerald morning.
Memories erased with insolent ease.
Hidden anguish churning in the subconscious,
Leaving me a silent witness
Bearing an irrational fear of the dark.

Pathways

Wake up, my friend.
Eternity is now.
Don't waste another minute on a doubt.
A thousand voices tell you,
"Don't believe your heart."
I am gonna tell you,
"It's time for you to start."
Believe the unbelievable.
Dreams are coming true.
The world our parents knew has passed away;
A new day is dawning.
There is magic in the air.
Come with me.
I think I know the way.
Let's be new pioneers
Of the frontier of our souls.
Take the path where others never go.
As long as you are with me,
I'm not afraid to try.
Listen to your heart;
I think you know.
Every day that is behind us
Has led us to right now,
A long and lonely journey
That we've known.
The future has been calling.
I am waiting, waiting, waiting
For you, my love.
I don't wanna go alone.

Lonely People

Today I met a man,
Years of sorrow in his eyes.
He looked so sad
It made me want to cry.
I wished that someone
Would take away his pain.
He just kept on walking
In the rain.
So much love is wasted
On those whose hearts are stone.
And so many gentle people
Live their lives alone.
Yet, we keep on searching,
Searching for a love come true.
That's what lonely people do.
I know from experience
'Cause I'm a lonely one, too.
Is love a lesson we must learn?
A privilege we earn?
The elusive pot of gold at Rainbow's End?
Is it fire and ice?
Is it sugar and spice?
Or a rare and quiet moment with a friend?
I want to tell the lonely ones,
"Don't give up your dreams!
Pretty soon they'll all be coming true.
Walk away from the pain
And start over again
'Til you find the love
That's waiting for you."

Midnight Calling

Night drags on to endless day.
My thoughts float like whispers
On the winds of memory.
Gentle touch of the poet
As soul touches soul,
Protecting me from the fierce unknown.
Strangers caught unaware
In fate's web, brought together
Into the mysterious universe
Of our hearts' longing.
Brief moments last eternities
When love ignites the soul.
Looking into your eyes
I saw myself
Gaining strength from love,
No longer frightened of what must be.
Lost in the pleasure
Of finding each other,
Forever captured in an instant,
A knight's reward for love unbound,
Joyously enslaved.
Half a world away and yet
I feel the warmth of your soul
Wrapped around me like a smile,
Saving me once again
From the emptiness I feel inside
As I waste another day
Without you.
I know you think of me
When the stars are bright beacons
Sending my love to you
On the darkest midnight canvas.
Songbirth, love's labor,

Melody of memories reborn
Reaches the depth of my soul,
Forever searching for your face
In a dream
I'll remember.

Timber

Memory brings me to that sanctuary,
The special place of my youth,
A haven of understanding,
Absorbing the turbulence and tears,
The anger aimed at unknown targets,
The volatile moods of adolescence.
With their quiet acceptance,
Soft and serene,
Tall oaks reassured me.
Life goes on.
Fear and anger passed quickly,
A flashflood of emotion.
Coming home to this family,
My stomach knots.
Tears cannot hide this sight.
My favorite Oak
Lies broken in the creek bed,
A brave and fallen soldier
In the battle of acid rain.
His comrades, Dogwood and Cedar,
Mourn with me as I turn away.
Leaving with the feeling, somehow,
I let my friends down.

Pan

A long-ago dream and far away,
Two lovers met, one yesterday,
Wild children freed from parents' looks
And captured in their storybooks.
The fire of youth danced in their eyes
As playful passions began to rise.
Love was born on a starry night
When two were one
On the midnight flight to Neverland.
Today those two do what they're told.
They forgot their vow to never grow old.
Each remembers a midnight dance,
But both are scared to take the chance
Just waiting on some fairy dust
To let them know just who to trust.
Is that true love behind that smile?
Or just the lure of a crocodile?
So neither one will make a stand
And both still dream of Neverland.

The Invisible Ones

Daylight breaks with a frigid blast.
My cardboard palace falls askew.
Layered in threadbare throwaways,
The daily trials begin anew.
Combing the paths of the rich ones
Who stare at me with open scorn.
I dirty up their neighborhood
With my clothing, ragged and torn.
Every day, I fight to survive.

I search for food or things to wear,
Digging through some bags and trashcans
For humble treasure buried there,
Greeting my brothers of the street,
Whose numbers grow from day to day.
We wish for some small bit of comfort.
Alley to street, we make our way.
Once a wife, with job and home
'Til too much drinking brought me down.
Swallowed pride asphyxiates me,
My heart as cold as the icy ground.
I pass by souls with lives of plenty.
They see our plight, yet look away.
Uncaring of my simplest needs,
They scurry to their busy day.
Trudging back to the cardboard city,
A rotting peach my only prize.
I hand it to a vagrant streetchild,
Cold anger in his sunken eyes.

Dark Moment

My mind is a void.
An empty, black vacuum
Of anti-thoughts,
Useless, trivial jargon,
Abundant nothingness.
Like a dictionary
In a blender,
A whirling mass
With no substance.
Trying to corral
This swirling vortex
Of nouns, adjectives, and verbs,

Reminds me of a leaky lifeboat
In a whirlpool
Of ambiguity.

Lost At Sea

I'll never forget the first time.
The first time I caught you looking at me
With eyes the color of a stormy sea.
I knew I'd never be the same.
I knew someone changed the rules of the game.
I've got to find my way back.
If it's the last thing I do,
I will find my way back to you.
'Cause I'm lost at sea,
Drifting with the tide,
Taking it in stride,
Taking everything that life throws at me.
I've got to hold on.
The current is strong.
It's taking me the long way home.
For once in my life,
I know where I'm going.
For once in my life,
I don't care where I've been.
I'm waiting for the light
To take me where I wanna be—
Back in your arms again,
Lost in your eyes,
Adrift on the sea of tranquillity,
Lost at sea,
Lost at sea.
I'm looking for a lover
Who's been looking for me.

I've got to hold on.
The current is strong.
It's taking me the long way home.

Night of Two Moons

The evening comes,
Two moons rising,
The ending of a perfect day.
Holding hands in the crystal city,
We watch the children play.
Running and growing
With the secrets they're knowing,
They'll find a better way.
Rainbow has children of her own.
Jason travels to the stars.
He said he'd bring us something back
Next time he visits Mars.
There are others I've never seen.
Even though we are apart,
I know they have a gentle soul
And, of course, a poet's heart.
Children of the universe
Underneath a foreign sun.
They're the promise of the future.
They belong to everyone.
Another day ending;
The love that I'm sending
Is love that I feel in return.
Sing me some tunes
Underneath these two moons.
I'm never too old to learn.

Song Without Music

Do you ever feel like a virtual stranger?
Always the one outside looking in,
Acutely aware of the inherent danger
Of being the lone wolf—a cardinal sin?
When I was young, "an imaginative child,"
Burdened by labels, the older I got.
Black sheep, a rebel,
A little too wild.
They'll never know that it hurt me, a lot.
Sweet understanding waits for me somewhere.
Somewhere there's someone who feels as I do.
We'll never know who we are
'Til we get there.
We'll never know if the story is true.
Like a song without music,
That's how I'm feeling—
Just a song with no music,
That's me, without you.
Give me the wings;
I'll soar like an eagle
Dancing on airwaves
So clear and so true.
Once we're together,
I think we'll uncover
A secret we've known from the start.
Don't be surprised when you discover
It's a song that you know by heart.

Incite Insight

The pulse of life,
The tidal seas,
The song is carried on the breeze.
The all that is
Calls out my name:
Instant change.
I look the same
But something's different,
It's plain to see.
Suddenly
My soul is free,
Like water breaking through a dam,
Understanding who I am.
Wait a minute...
Can it be?
The miracle of love
Is me!

Index

A

abductees, 2, 7, 107, 124, 128, 150
abductions, 3, 73, 105, 107, 122, 125, 158
Accelerated learning capacity, 174
alcohol, 128
aliens (see also grays, reptilians), 4, 11, 18-22, 24, 25, 30, 33, 35-37, 41, 42, 52, 55, 60, 61, 86, 88, 93-95, 109, 123, 125, 126, 128, 129, 134, 141, 157, 159, 160, 182
angel hair, 80
animal mutilations, 105, 165, 173
Ark, The, 152, 155
Armageddon, 169
asteroid impacts, 151
atomic reverberation in vacuum, 177

B

babies, 41, 42, 54, 56, 61, 87, 88, 103, 187, 190, 193, 194
Baton Rouge, 65
bioplasm, 80
Bo and Peep (see also Heaven's Gate suicide), 154
Bob, 65-67, 69
Booger Eyes, 96
Branson, 4, 145
Brogan, Jean, 39, 60, 69
broken man, 9, 18, 20

C

California, 153
cape, 86, 182
carcinogens, 162, 164
Challenger, 73
chromator, 67
chromosome splicing (see also genetic restructuring), 171, 173
Clinton, President Bill, 129
colonization, 110
colostrum, 162
comedy, 82
Communion, 4
Crawford, Forest, 103
crop formations, 172
crystal city, 62
cut, 10, 22

D

dark matter, 175
"Davis, Kathie" (see Kauble, Debbie Jordan)
depression, 128, 133
desensitizing, 168
devil, 56
dimensional doorways, 115, 119
dimensions, 177
disinfectant, 88, 188
DNA, 79, 110, 119, 172, 173-176

E

earth changes, 119, 139, 151, 152, 162, 163

Index

Easter Island, 119
Equinox, 140
evacuations, 163

F

fear year, 122, 124, 135, 147
fibroplasia, 173

G

genetic restructuring (see also
    chromosome splicing), 174
Georgia, 73
God, 27, 28, 56, 131, 134, 135,
    138, 140, 141, 147, 158, 180
Grandpa (see also "Queetzal,")
    19, 20, 86, 182
gravitational waves, 177
grays, 30, 42, 53, 55, 61, 66-68,
    71, 86, 88, 93-95, 123, 126,
    157, 158, 182
Great Battle, 140
Great Veil, 139
Greenpeace, 78
Guardians, 110
gynecological procedures, 21, 25,
    31, 43, 46, 53, 86, 95

H

Hale-Bopp comet, 153, 155
Haley, Leah A., 106, 107
Heaven's Gate suicide, 153, 154
Hendrix, Jimi, 40
Hickson, Charles, 77
high command council, 171
Hill, Betty, 77

Hopkins, Budd, 3, 4, 5, 6, 25, 105
Howe, Linda Moulton, 105
Hussain, Saddam, 169
hybrids, 36, 41, 42, 54, 61, 63,
    166
hypnosis, 6, 7, 10, 13, 17, 18, 22,
    38, 48, 51, 65, 69, 123, 145,
    181

I

immobilization, 113
implants, 81, 165
incubators, 187
Indiana, 143
indoctrination, 113, 167, 176
Intellectual capacity, increase in,
    174
interdimensional shift, 115
intervention, 113, 117
Intruders, 3, 4, 5, 78, 102

J

Jeremiah, 138
Jesus Christ, 27, 135, 138, 139,
    140
Jet Propulsion Laboratory, 162

K

Kauble, Debbie Jordan, 2, 4, 77,
    101, 103, 105, 143, 144, 145
Koresh, David, 131, 147

L

Lamour, Louis, 59
League of Controllers, 114, 118,

Index

League of Controllers (continued)
120, 121, 125, 169
life span, increase in, 174
Light Horse, 140
lights, 14, 21, 30, 81, 86, 93, 140,
143, 144, 174
liquid, 61
Louisiana, 66, 71
LSD, 146

M

manipulation of consciousness,
114
mask, 11
matter transference, 81
Mexico, 57
Midwestern United States, 163
missing time, 3
Mississippi, 60
Missouri, 4, 60, 101, 103-105,
123, 145
molecular changes, 81
Moody Blues, 103
music, 82
mutations, 161, 172

N

National Guard, 57, 130
Native Americans, 28
near-death experiences, 31
New Madrid fault, 151
new world federation, 111
nosebleeds, 72
nuclear war, 27, 112, 162

O

out-of-body experiences (OBEs),
150
odors, 52, 85, 87, 112, 187
Oklahoma City bombing, 146,
147
Omni magazine, 3
one-world government, 167
oxygen depletion, 162, 164
Ozark Mountains, 60, 123
ozone depletion, 112

P

Palermo, Jo, 103
phobias, 4
photolytic beams, 165
photon diffusion, 79, 80
photosynthesis, 82, 162, 171
pig, 4, 10
Pleiadians, 166
pole shift, 162
pollution, 163, 173
poltergeist activity, 73, 74, 149
prayer, 135, 138, 139, 147
praying mantis type alien, 171
promiscuity, 4
psychic abilities, 73
psychological tests, 72
Pyramid of the Sun, 57
pyramids, 57, 62, 102

Q

Queetzal, 54-59, 87, 88, 89, 185

Index

R

Rainbow, 42, 43, 62, 66, 68
rapes, 32, 33, 36
reptilians, 52, 53, 125, 126, 127
Richter scale, 139
robot-like hand, 18, 19
Rock of Presidents, 119

S

scars, 4, 13
scientific socialization, 168
screen memories, 6
seance, 40
semen, 32, 36, 124
SETI, 114
sex, 31, 36, 93, 125, 126
smoke alarm, 14
souls of light, 140
sounds, 14, 40, 86, 88, 112, 144, 193
spectral transport, 81
spiritual awakening, 115, 116, 119
spiritual growth, 8, 115, 120
St. Louis, 101, 103-105
Stonehenge, 119
storms, 139, 163
Strategic Defense Initiative (SDI), 120
Strieber, Whitley, 4
subliminal programming, 117
surveillance, 167

T

telepathic communications, 78, 79
Teotihuacan, 57, 119
test subjects, 165
theater, 82
threats, 125, 126, 129
time fluctuation, 178
transmogrification, 112
transplantation of species, 112
triggering effect, 3
Trilobites, 55

U

UFOs, 3, 5, 17, 21, 24, 29, 31, 40, 60, 61, 66, 80, 81, 86, 87, 105, 109, 126, 129, 130, 140, 143, 145, 154, 162, 170
Union of Soviet Socialist Republics, 167, 168
united consciousness, 140
US Army, 56

V

veil of secrecy, 111
virtual reality, 146
volcanic eruptions, 139

W

Waco, Texas, 131, 147
Walton, Travis, 77
World Trade Center bombing, 131, 146

Z

Zanopria the Elder, 171

The Book Shopper

A Division of Greenleaf Publications

So busy that you cherish every second of leisure time?
Want someone else to take care of unpleasant tasks for you?
Loathe traffic, crowds, and waiting in line?
Lack transportation?
Stumped every time you must buy a gift for someone?

Never fear! The Book Shopper® *is here!*

We established our company with your needs in mind. You can now buy books by simply dialing our toll-free number. We'll ship right to your home or work place! *We'll even gift wrap or ship to a third party at no extra charge if you like!*

📖 Novels 📖 Cookbooks 📖 Romances 📖 Westerns

📖 Children's books 📖 Sports Books 📖 Any kind of book!*

1-800-905-8367

(615-896-1549 outside the U.S.)